Calm Social Media

don't be a social media puppet!

Vishnu Goyal

ISBN: 978-93-5311-956-0

Cover designed by Vishnu Goyal
(with design help of *Ivy Sabado* & *Reychelle Ann Ignacio* from *Canva*)

Disclaimer

Every effort has been made to avoid errors or mistakes in this book. In spite of this, errors might have crept in as this book is not made by robots, but human beings. In case you come across any mistake, error or discrepancy (including grammatical ones), you may notify the author about it, which shall be taken care of in the next edition. Neither the author, nor the publisher & seller will be responsible for any direct, consequential, or incidental damages arising out of the use of this book.

Vishnu Goyal

Visit my website at www.VishnuGoyal.com

Calm Social Media

Visit Calm Social Media website at www.CalmSocialMedia.com

Dedicated to work-in-progress
of building a Carefree World...

Social media sucks only those who allowed it to.

—VISHNU GOYAL

Contents

Preface

Social Media can be best & worst at the same time depending on how you use it. Today one of the greatest concerns of all (leaving unaware people aside) is Social Media. There is lot of anxiety over it. Some people are not able to study, some are not able to sleep, some are harassed, some are depressed, some are exposed to cyber bullying, some are losing quality time, some are suffering from FOMO (Fear of Missing Our), some are losing relationships, some are going under debt, some are losing their minds, some are suffering from physical disability and the list of negativities goes on...

But the reason for all of this is one – "***Social Media Abuse***". It's not social media but the abuse of social media by people! People have created so much buzz around social media and most of it is negative. We just need to calm it & it's in our hands. After all, Social Media can't be more powerful than its creators - we, the human beings, right?

Calm Social Media book is an effort to sum up all of my social media understanding coupled with data from others' studies, research & statistics as well about the subject to make you aware about alarming social media statistics, studies, research & social media issues affecting billions of lives (including yours) I am concerned about, possible cure & solutions to those problems, help you use social media in a more sensible manner & at the best, Calm Social Media. Hopefully, this book will help you understand how social media is affecting your daily life, how it impacts you in short as well as long run, how can you make best use of it and lead a life of more freedom with more quality time, do some more productive tasks and make your life much better in toto. As of now you may be behind "*social media bars*" but after finishing this book, you will have your freedom back with you.

One more thing...

... I have tried to make this book as small & crisp as possible while still containing all the stuff I was eager to deliver. I believe there must be many more things on the subject that you are aware about, but I am not & therefore, not included in the book. You can help me & the entire Calm Social Media community with your feedback, suggestions, criticism or appreciation. You can reach me directly at Vishnu@CalmSocialMedia.com. I will try to incorporate your valuable suggestions in the next edition of this book.

Further, to stay tuned with Calm Social Media, visit CalmSocialMedia.com anytime & feel free to subscribe for email updates. You'll not be disappointed. All Calm Social Media's content will save you more time than you will spend on consuming it. That's my promise.

Note: While this book deals with social media issues in general life & the solutions to tackle them, it also deals a bit about the issues related to smartphones, internet & other matters, as social media is not a problem in isolation & it's important to discuss & deal with its essential ingredients, ingredients which make social media complete & without which social media can't exist!

Acknowledgment

To realize my idea of writing a book on social media that can improve the life of people all around the world and help them make better social media & internet habits and to bring this book to life, a thorough research has been conducted. I have made a limited use of data curated from hundreds of researches, studies, articles & other sources (hereinafter referred as "sources") keeping in mind the "*Fair Use Doctrine*". At all places, appropriate credit has been given to the concerned sources. If any credit is left, that is purely un-intentional. You can let me know about it by simply dropping a mail at Vishnu@CalmSocialMedia.com and I will correct my sillies in the next edition!

I would like to specially acknowledge the contribution of *MediaKix* & *dscout* for allowing me to use their infographic & report on "*How Much Time Do People Spend on Social Media?*" & "*Mobile touches: a study on humans and their tech*" respectively.

Further, I have used excerpt from my own articles published on my own network of sites. I own full rights over that data and have rightfully used as much data as I thought required for this book. Sites include CalmSocialMedia.com, crunch.WinfiY.com, ROLLZIGN.com, among others.

Special Thanks To...

My mother, Smt. Bimla Goyal – for selflessly loving & caring me & always aiding me in all decisions of my life.

My father, Shri Ramesh Goyal – for giving me freedom to do what I want to and scolding me for my wrongdoings.

My loving brother, Tarun – for saving time from his busy schedule to read the very first to final version of this book, providing critical feedback & believing in me more than I do in myself.

All my sisters - for their endless support, good wishes & putting my interest even before their own.

Alka Ma'am - for blessing me with her innumerable guidance; advice; leadership & experience during my CA-articleship which helps me a lot in pursuing my own path.

You - for giving your valuable time to read this book.

Notes to Make Your Calm Social Media Experience Even Better...

- I am not an author by education & I have taken full liberty out of it! I wrote this book the way I like to read & the way I talk. I have used the conversation tone so that you don't feel like I'm "talking to the air" (I'm talking to you, of course). I have also worked "a few extra" to ensure that you don't use Calm Social Media book to make yourself sleep!

- To make proper conversation with you, I have used "*you*" at times in the book! Instances can be there in the book, where you will not fit in. Don't blame me for that, as anomalies are always there, right?

- Read this book in the same order in which it has been arranged, as the information is connected from starting to end. If you jump at another section before finishing the previous ones, you'll not be able to understand Calm Social Media in way you must understand. So, don't skip anything & don't jump from one section to another, as entire information is connected.

- In case you are reading a physical copy of this book, you can go to CalmSocialMedia.com to easily refer the links mentioned in the "*References*" placed at the end of this book as links in a paper are obviously not clickable!

- At some points, words can be harsh, as *sugar coated words* will not be able to get the way I want to deal with harsh issues and the way I want you to feel about those issues. So, be ready for it!

1.0 Introduction: The Idea Behind Calm Social Media

1.1 How It All Started?

Well, before delving into the idea behind "*Calm Social Media*", I would like to discuss my educational background and the timing of this idea that will help you understand the idea behind "*Calm Social Media*".

I enrolled in Indian Chartered Accountancy ("CA") Course in April 2013, studied Accountancy and Taxation for around 4 years and cleared 2 levels of the examination (after failing for 2 times at the second level) along with 3 years of training (will not bore you with too much academics as I know it's boring for you to read such stuff and you are not here for that, right?).

During my CA course, I was developing my interest in Web Designing & Content Writing (that I enjoy even now) & start developing websites alongside my CA training. For my CA final examinations, I took a leave of 4 months. While those 4 months were meant to be used for my studies, I did just another thing & that was the time when the story of Calm Social Media began!

1.2 Genesis of Calm Social Media

During those 4 months, I was coming up with many website ideas and in excitement, I purchased a whopping of more than 100 domains in toto (totally nonsense as far as business is concerned) and I started creating social profiles for all my new business brands (all my final examination books were going dusty when I was busy creating new sites and social media profiles!). It took a couple of weeks and I was having more than 120 social profiles that included more than 41 Facebook pages, around 40 twitter accounts, 30 Instagram accounts and few Pinterest, Google+ and Tumblr profiles (well there is no harm in that as all of them were created for my businesses, right?)

Although I never used social media much for my personal use, but when I created my own corner on the Internet (VishnuGoyal.com), I was giving lots of attention to my personal social profiles. I started frequently posting on Twitter, Facebook and other profiles. I was frequently checking how many likes, comments and shares I was getting. I was checking my followers for countless number of times. It was not later when I realized that instead of making blog posts for my business blogs, I was spending more time on just checking for useless notifications on my Twitter and Facebook profiles. It was a kinda compulsion & I felt "*addicted to social media*".

Just after that realization, I googled "*Social Media Addiction*" & got to know that I am not alone! I became a part of the crowd which is facing the same problem. I was stunned when I got to know that "***social media sites like Facebook and Twitter are more addictive than cigarettes & alcohol***".[1]

That was the day when I decided to limit my social media time. I started thinking about how should I go about it? Thanks to my self - discipline, I disabled Facebook in my smartphone (Facebook being a system app can't be uninstalled!), logged out of my personal accounts in other social media apps (twitter, Instagram, Pinterest and Tumblr; never used Snapchat). I installed Facebook Pages Manager to manage my business pages and kept my business accounts logged in other social media apps; turned off all these apps' notifications and decided a fixed time to deal with even my business social media accounts (more details later!).

After doing all this stuff, I became more curious about Social Media Addiction and after doing little research on the issue, concluded that improper use of social media is creating many problems in our lives & perhaps those problems outweigh the social media's good deeds too. It was clear to me that improper use of social media is literally destroying us (or better, we are destroying ourselves with *Social Media Ab-use*) & I must do something about it.

Although, the information was accessible on the web, but it was scattered on different corners of the web. Further, I couldn't find a source where all social media issues are handled in one place. So, I decided to create one & make people like you aware about the *social media issues* (which is a little known yet a very big & serious life problem now) & how you can deal with it.

I started digging the issues deeper; researched on other social media life problems; did some social media experiments of my own (discussed in later sections), collated all the data & my experience in the form of a book & got it published to spread the message to you. All this process thrilled me...

... To get started, I decided to finalize the name of the book & design a website (CalmSocialMedia.com) for it (for early promotion of the book &.... my love for web designing, of course!).

1.3 Calm Social Media: The Nomenclature

People are cutting on their sleep time to have more & more of social media, making their eyes bear pain with increased social media wall time, advancing their travel plans for a perfect "*Insta-Pic*" & what's not! I think people, brands, companies (& everybody & anybody else you can think of) are creating a lot of buzz on social media. We just need to calm it! Simple thing, right? That simple thing is the basis of nomenclature: "*Calm Social Media*"! Appropriate! Isn't it? Do let me know your thoughts at Vishnu@CalmSocialMedia.com.

1.4 Calm Social Media & Plus

Initially I decided to write only about social media. Later, with my ongoing research on the topic, I realized that Social Media can't be dealt with as a single topic and our gadgets & internet must be there.

To make it happen, I expanded my research & experience to have a take on our internet, gadgets & most importantly, our smartphone habits (I call it 'Plus' here). Although the nomenclature of the book is 'Calm Social Media", we'll discuss related issues as well in lite-mode with focus on social media! Isn't great? (I hope you said yes!)

1.5 What You Can Expect from Calm Social Media Book?

Here, I would like to tell you that I am managing my business social profiles for about 3 years now. For the same time, I am consuming more & more research & studies on social media. I have also done a few experiments of my own. But, I don't label myself a Social Media Expert! Since most people (perhaps you too) skip the preface part, so I would like to repeat that this book is an effort to sum up all of my social media understanding coupled with data from others' studies, research & statistics as well about the subject to make you aware about alarming social media statistics, studies, research & social media issues affecting billions of lives (including yours) I am concerned about, possible cure & solutions to those problems, help you use social media in a more sensible manner & at the best, Calm Social Media.

Hopefully, this book will help you understand how social media is affecting your daily life, how it impacts you in short as well as long run, how can you make best use of it and lead a life of more freedom with more quality time, do some more productive tasks and make your life much better in toto. As of now you may be behind social media bars but after finishing this book, you will have your freedom back with you.

Before we proceed to Calm Social Media, I would also like to make one thing clear: It is fine for bloggers, marketers, brands and other persons to use social media for as much time as they need, as they use social media as part of their work & in that case we need to see it from a different perspective. As a web designer, content writer and social media manager for lots of my own brands, I spent hours each day on social media but that's a different matter. Calm Social Media addresses the issues that Social Media or better, "*Social Media Abuse*" (will discuss this term later) causes in your life from personal usage perspective & not from the perspective of marketing. I hope I'm clear.

Further, in creation of this book, facts & results of various social media researches & studies have been used. All such studies are conducted on sampling basis & may not represent the entire population. So, the results thereof can't be generalized & the same may vary with different set of users.

Let's hit start now...

2.0 Social Media – Good or Bad?

Today, we all use social networking sites & messaging applications like Facebook, Twitter, Instagram, LinkedIn, Pinterest, Google+, YouTube, Snapchat ("Social Media"). We use social media for chatting, getting news, discover new places, get in touch with our friends & family, for work, express ourselves & a lot of other activities! You know that. Did you ever think is it good or bad to use social media? How does it impact you, your health, your career & other aspects of your life?

Well, this is the very first question that need to be answered before we proceed to understand rest of the social media matters. Is it good or bad to use social media? As far as my experience is concerned, I believe that there is no harm in using social media. Good or bad depends on how you use it, how much time you spend on it, for what purpose you use it.

Social media is not bad! It has given a new voice to democracy, where all people are equal, have right to express themselves & reach crores of people out there.

As long as social media is in your control, you are good to go. But if you are in control of social media, that's a problem you need to tackle. Here, I want to tell you a real-life incidence from my commute of home to office...

... Just like yet another training day of mine, I was going to office via metro, enjoying metro-travel & reading a kindle book. After some time, when I looked around for a break from screen-time, I noticed two wonderful young guys sitting in front of me (on seat reserved for Senior Citizens!). One of them was restless picking up his phone every few seconds & just checking if there was new notification. I thought, the guy was really waiting for something urgent over phone. But I was wrong. Soon, that guy asked his friend very anxiously:

> *"अरे यार आधे घंटे से कोई नया मैसेज क्यों नहीं आ रहा है?"*
> *[English: "why I'm not getting any new messages for the last half hour?"]*

... I gazed at that guy's phone. He was having his phone unlocked, frequently juggling through various WhatsApp chats without any new messages!

That incidence shocked me a little bit. Does checking your WhatsApp so frequently is really that important? Anyway, I just found a new "*social media patient*". I wanted to talk with that guy about social media issue, but before I could do that, metro reached my destination & I needed to de-board! Bad luck! Anyway, it's one of the finest examples of Social Media Abuse & in particular, Social Media Addiction.

Coming to the question "whether Social Media is good or bad?", I think answer to this does lie in a quote (& it's one of my favorites!) which goes like this:

> *"Life sucks only those who allowed it to" – Unknown*

> *(If you know who said this, please let me know with proper source!)*

As far as the social media issue is concerned, I can answer the above question with just a little modification in the above quote. For social media, it will go like this:

> *"Social media sucks only those who allowed it to" – Vishnu Goyal*

As far as the impact of social media is concerned, people have mixed views about it. In a teen social media study conducted by *Pew Research Center*, 31% participants said that social media's impact is mostly positive, 24% said it's mostly negative, while 45% said it's neutral! While these results can't be generalized, but these serve as an indicator of how mixed perception people have about social media.[2]

We all live in a free world where we enjoy the liberty to take our own decisions. Our social media decisions are not in hands of social media companies or the people leading them, but in our hands.

You are the creator of your social media story. You control how much time you spend on social media. If you can't take a break, you are at fault. No one is putting gun to your head & forcing you to spend time on social media. It's your choice, your decision. You know it's doing no good to you, but you keep on doing that. So, be a wiser user of social media. Just outsmart it!

At this point, I would also like to quote a few lines from the song "*Walk on Water*" by "*Jason Crabb*":

"It's the path you take
The steps you make
That make you who you are"

Each time I listen to this song, I realize how true these words are! You can learn a lesson from these words of wisdom. It also supports my opinion that it's not social media which is bad, the bad lies within us. We need to make ourselves good.

So, it would not be wrong to conclude that Social Media is neither good nor bad. It depends on how we use it. *Social Media* has many good things, but *Social Media Abuse* is a "*problem-mine*"! *Social Media* is a blessing, but *Social Media Abuse* is curse. *Social Media* is good, but our "*ab-use*" of it makes it bad. So, we just need to stop abusing social media & convert "*ab-use*" to just "*good-use*"!

What exactly is Social Media Abuse & what problems it is creating? We'll explore. Before going there, let's understand the two sides of social media...

3.0 Two Sides of Social Media

Social Media has two sides - one is personal and the other is professional/ business.

I will come to the second aspect first i.e. business. In today's online world, lots of people are using social media to make a business out of it. Professional users include professional bloggers, celebrities (rather social media celebrities), small to big businesses, among others.

Now, managing social media accounts of corporates & celebrities is a full-time job. These people spend hours every day on social media to engage with customers & admirers, reply to their queries & even provide online solutions through social media.

Social Media is part of their job & it can't be treated as addiction, right? It's professional approach to social media.

Another aspect of social media is personal one i.e. using social media for sharing personal things, sharing opinions & ideas, "*stay connected*", et cetera.

Well, there is no harm in personal use of social media, but the problem is when you care about how many likes, comments & followers you are getting!

You ignore the real moments in life just to capture them in your smartphone so that those can be shared on your social media profiles...

... That's not enough. You keep constantly checking the reaction on your posts, finding it impossible to resist the temptation. That's a kinda social media "*obsession*" or "*addiction*" (will know the difference later) - a position where you have no control on your social media actions.

You need to understand that while using social media personally, you can't devote hours to curate content, create content & post it just to satisfy your social media ego. If you are so eager for doing that, learn it professionally and become a social media manager. Convert your hobby in your work. That's a good approach.

If you are pursuing other career or are good at something else, then take steps to limit your social media use. I personally think, 10 minutes a day is more than enough for social media.

And yeah... don't stress your mind about what can you do to control it! While we proceed further, we will discuss Calm Social Media tips, tricks & steps in detail. So, just reax & enjoy your reading!

Now you understand whether social media is good or bad, two sides of social media. Great accomplishment! Congrats! Now it's time to learn about Social Media Abuse. Let's proceed...

4.0 Social Media Abuse

4.1 What's Social Media Abuse?

Social Media Abuse includes "No-brainer, excessive, improperly-regulated, profit-oriented, selfish, inhuman, abusive & underage use of social media. Social Media abuse has created a wide range of new problems & issues for all of us. Social Media Abuse is destroying you without even letting you know that you are being destroyed!

"Social Media Abuse" is the problem in formation of which social media users as well as social media companies & their leaders, all have contributed. In disguise of 'providing a platform for sharing', few social media companies going ways beyond ethics, humanity & social responsibility but the money. In the chase of more and more money, all services are frequently updated to provide you with so-called better user experience which is nothing but an effort to keep you hooked for a longer period of time so that you can "*waste*" more time on these platforms.

We, as users, have our contribution as well to the problem of Social Media Abuse! We just start a 5-minute quick look to see what's going on with our friends, family, in our country and around the world. However, when those 5 minute gets converted into the hours of scrolling, we didn't even realize. People are using social media services for illegal businesses, spreading fake news, spamming, broadcasting inhuman videos, stalking random people including children & all kinds of abusive things!

For students, their study is getting destroyed, for adults their career and relationships are getting complex. Today Social Media Abuse is impacting your health, career, children, job, studies, businesses & all other aspects of life in negative ways & we need to act on it.

People sacrifice their sleep and quality time that they could spend with their real friends and abandon the family-fun just for the sake of sharing more & getting few more likes or a few more retweets from some fake friends and fake followers.

If you are here, chances are you are among those 220-crore people who use Facebook. You will agree with me that most of the content shared on Facebook are just "*pieces of nonsense*".

In spite of that, you just can't stop yourself from tapping the social media icons in your phone and start scrolling. You have no time to think. This is how Social Media Abuse is killing your creativity and real happiness. The time you could spend in real conversation with real people is spent in having online chat with people who you never meet in person.

You need to know one thing that online friends are no more than virtual friends (leaving few exceptions aside). In case you need help, these fake friends will not be of any help but the real friends.

4.2 Illustrative List of Problems Caused by Social Media Abuse

Problems discussed above are just few branches of Social Media Abuse. I would like to make a non-exhaustive list of problems caused by Social Media Abuse here...

- Social Media Obsession & Addiction
- Oversharing: Reading Less, Sharing More
- Social Media Bullying & Harassment – A Part of Cyberbullying
- Use of Social Media by Underaged or Small Children
- Sharenting
- Negative Health Caused by Social Media Including Blindness, Anxiety, Unhappiness, Stress, Sleep Deprivation, Depression, et cetera
- Peer Pressure & Inferiority Complex
- FOMO: Fear of Missing Out
- Information Overload, Unfocused Life & Short Attention Span
- Education & Career Harm
- Distractions: Work & Productivity Loss
- Instant Gratification Issue
- Financial Crisis & Indebtedness
- No Free Time: Lost Creativity & Intelligence
- Brain Depreciation
- Fake News & Rumors
- Hate Speech & Violence
- Suicidal Thoughts & Deaths
- Social Media Trolling
- Others: There are many...

4.3 Is It Really Something You Need to Be Worried About?

How much serious the problem of Social Media Abuse is? Well, the availability of programs like "*Internet Addiction Rehab Program*[3]" says it all!

You may think of social media just as a tool of fun, a medium to express yourself & remain connected with your loved ones and blah, blah, blah! But the fact is that time you spent on social media impacts your mind, health, studies, creativity, sleep, mentality, career & lots of other important aspects of your life. I think "*Social Media Abuse*" has become a serious disease now especially for younger generation & it has to be dealt with seriously to avoid the harmful outcomes of it!

In the subsequent sections, you will get to know how much negative impact you are having from Social Media Abuse & what you can do to cure yourself & others as well. Before doing that, let's discuss one very important thing – Why? Why you should Calm Social Media? Let's start...

5.0 Why? Why You Should Calm Social Media?

While there are many reasons for why you should quit social media or at least cut your time on it. Here are a few of them to help you get started...

▪ It Makes You Happier

Every person who quit social media, find himself/herself happier! They are less anxious & depressed. Going offline makes people happy. You'll face less negativity & your mindset will be positive[4].

▪ You'll Have More Time

You spend hours daily on Facebook, Twitter, Instagram, WhatsApp, Snapchat & other apps for no good reason. If you cut your time on these apps, you will be left with much more time & the life will not be too short to pursue other things you love! Just think about what you can do if you have at least 2 hours extra per day! I think you can do a lot with that time, right? With Calm Social Media, you'll have fewer distractions & will be more productive.

▪ You'll Be Away from Fake World

Much of the moments shared on social media are far away from daily life. On social media, everybody seems to be happy! Have you seen people posting a sad photo of themselves? I guess, no! All wants to show-off that they are living a happy life, no matter what's going in their real life. Want an example? Okay! Have a look at this tweet (thanks to MakeUseof.com[5] for reporting this):

> There *are* some celebrities that make scheduled posts (for whatever reason), and it's likely done to make them seem relevant or cool. Consider Paris Hilton's Tweet that happened **shortly after she was arrested on cocaine charges**: '*In bed watching Family Guy. Love this show! So hilarious! Stewie is my favorite :) love his accent."*

[An unreal post in the fake world of social media]

As reported by MakeUseof.com, this tweet on Paris Hilton's Twitter account came out shortly after she was arrested on cocaine charges! Obviously, "*she was not in bed watching Family Guy*", as the tweet suggests!

This is just one example! Everything seems "cool" on social media but it's not. With a look at the above image, you can trust me, right? You are victim of such fake online world & feel yourself of a loser. If you Calm Social Media, you'll have no social media, no fake world, no guilty feeling.

▪ You'll Have More to Talk About

In the world of social media, you share quite every important moment of your life on your public profiles. Be it your new job, your vacation photos, your today's dinner plan & blah, blah, blah! Due to this trend, everybody knows what's going on in your life & when they meet you, neither they have much to ask, nor you have much to tell! I think sharing less on social media leaves you with more stuff to talk about when you meet people.

▪ Benefits Are Endless ...

Calm Social Media benefits are endless! Literally, endless. Would be better for us to stop here & dive into Social Media Abuse problems & solutions right now. Don't worry, I would keep discussing other benefits of "*quitting & cutting*" social media as we proceed!

Let's Calm Social Media together...

6.0 Social Media Addiction

6.1 What's Social Media Obsession, Addiction & Anxiety

People are spending more time than ever on social media. Result is a dedicated term in the world of social media problems called "*Social Media Addiction*". It's a situation of "*Compulsive Social Media Use*" where you feel compelled to use social media & you can't stop yourself from doing so.

Study[6] by Royal Society for Public Health, UK, found that "***social media sites like Facebook and Twitter are more addictive than cigarettes & alcohol!***"

Excessive use of Social Media leading to a point of compulsion can be considered as *Social Media Addiction*. It's a situation where you feel forced to use social media.

For example, if you can't stop yourself from checking your Facebook or Twitter, probably you're an addict because you're not able to control your social media cravings. That means you are in control of social media. The best way to describe Social Media Addiction:

"It's a situation when you forget that Social Media is for you to use & it's not for the social media to use you"

I hope I have clearly described what Social Media Addiction is.

If you get frustrated when you can't check your Facebook, Instagram, Twitter or WhatsApp account, it's a sign of *Social Media Addiction*. It's also called "*Social Media Anxiety Disorder*".

The more you use social media, more are the chances of having anxiety disorders.[7] I'm not saying so, but the research!

Study suggests that "*addiction to social networks on the Internet may be a potential mental health problem for some users*".[8] Anxiety & Depression Association of America reported[9]:

> *"almost 20% of people with social media accounts cannot go more than three hours without checking them... those who have social media anxiety disorder, just being away from their Facebook or Twitter account for a few minutes can cause severe anxiety."*

These reports make it clear that Social Media Addiction is a serious issue.

Today, we have become so much emotionally connected to social media that most of us can't even think of deleting our social media accounts. You can't spend a day without social media & if you have too, you find it very hard. Remember last time when you checked your social media? Probably "*just moments ago*" is the answer you'll get! And if you check your phone or other device at the moment, perhaps you will find social media notifications waiting for your attention.

Most important point of Social Media Addiction is that many people want to restrict the time they spend on social media, on games, but they are not able to do so. That's what addiction is!

People, who joined social media just for "time-pass" are now hooked to it even in their "work-time". That's addiction.

You're at home with your loved ones but you can't stop yourself from checking your Facebook – That's addition.

You need to submit that assignment by EOD, but you need to check the WhatsApp message that just arrived from one of your friends – That's addiction.

Your eyes are turning red for sleep, but you need to check what's new in your twitter feed – That's addiction.

You have your exam next day, but you are chatting mindlessly with your friends because you think it's "*cool*" – That's addiction!

Well, the examples of Social Media Addiction are countless. These examples make it crystal clear how social media has created a perfect "***work-life-im-balance***" in our lives. Forget the real happiness. Everything is virtual now!

Our overuse of social media & internet has resulted in some realities, which are fun for some people while ridiculous & jealous for others!

Today list of internet & social media celebrities doesn't include only people but cats & dogs as well! People are spending hours watching photos & videos of cats, dogs & other pets!

It reminds me of "*Jiffpom*" - who is the most famous dog & animal in the world[10]. Jiffpom has followers perhaps more than your favorite celebrity or brand & you can feel jealous on knowing his fan count! Jiffpom is 3-times *Guinness World Record Holder*, most followed animal on Instagram with over 8.1 million followers, and has a whopping fan following of 25 million across all social media networks. After all this, he is just a dog!

Well, I have no issues with animals. I quoted the example of Jiffpom to show that for even interacting with animals, we are using internet & social media. You see their videos, their photos, like them, comment on them, share them! When totaled, all of this takes a lot of time. If instead of doing that, you spend time in a zoo, or playing with pets of your own or your neighbors, it will be worthier!

In the world of social media, if you tell somebody that you are not on Facebook or WhatsApp, it will be the most surprising thing for them. I have faced this situation. Let me tell you about that incidence.

It happened in November 2014! I just completed my Chartered Accountancy Intermediate Examinations & joined the Final Examination classes on the very next day. Within a week time, I had couple of "*class-friends*" there. One of them asked me for my WhatsApp No. to share notes but "*fortunately*" I didn't have one! I used to use only email & text messaging then. Surely, I replied I don't have a WhatsApp account. That guy was shocked to know that, and he uttered these words:

> *"भाई, तू जिंदा कैसे है?"*
> [English: *Brother, how are you even alive?*]

... Well, I still remember my answer. And back then also, I was as confident as I am today, because I know, I was on the right path. I asked him to mail the notes & thankfully he did! I got the notes on email...

... Being on WhatsApp at that time was more of a loss than a benefit for me. So, I opt for the right option. I didn't care what others think of me & I don't care what others think of me.

I always remember: Social Media is made for our use. We are not made for the use of social media. So, if you are not active on social media, good for you. Don't care about what others think of you. People will come & go. Your learning stays with you...

... We all know what is shared on 'most' of the WhatsApp groups, be it a friends group, colleague groups or any other group. As per my "guesstimates", 90% of the WhatsApp communication doesn't worth our time. Well, that's not only our fault, right? Sometimes, we are forced to be on WhatsApp since our family is there, our friends & business contacts are there. So, we are forced to be there. Same was the case for me...

... Within my training period of 3 years, I don't know for how many times I have installed & uninstalled WhatsApp! I personally don't like it (the app is good, but the way people are using it, is not!).

I made the recent uninstall on May 2, 2018. Okay? I forgot we're talking about Social Media Addiction here! So, let's keep my WhatsApp experiment for another section and talk about Social Media Addiction here...

6.2 How Much Time Do You Spend on Social Media?

People who get addicted to Social Media can spend hours of their day on the different networks. If you ask them how much time they spend on it, they can lie about it. It can also lead to severe health issues like eye-strain due to increased screen time, neck pain (since your head is in your gadget for majority of the time), depression, laziness, cut in physical activities, et cetera.

'*Except if you are an exception*', on average, you spend 40 minutes on YouTube, 35 minutes on Facebook, 25 minutes on Snapchat, 15 minutes on Instagram & just 1 minute on Twitter. Have a look at this infographic...

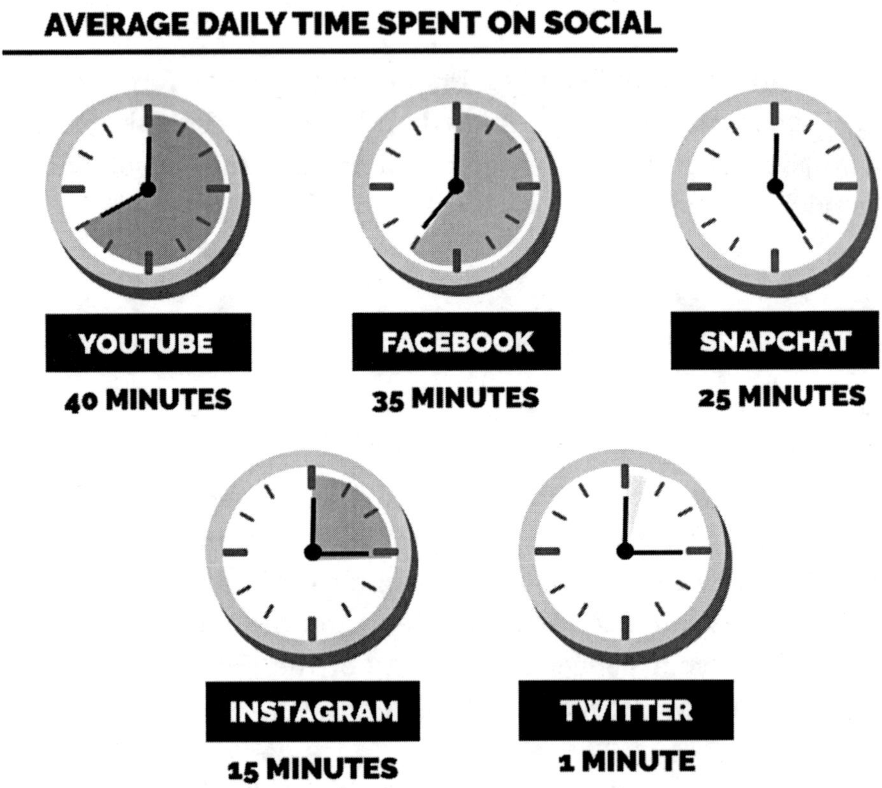

[Average Daily Time Spent on Social Media – Infographic by Mediakix]

The total comes at 116 minutes or we can simply say 2 hours. It is the average time spent on social media by each person in one day. Yeah... you might be spending less or more time (that only you know!) but average is 2 hours.[11]

Interestingly, Mediakix[12], an Influencer Marketing Agency, calculated an estimate of total time spent on social media in a lifetime & the figure is 5 years, 4 months! Huge, right?

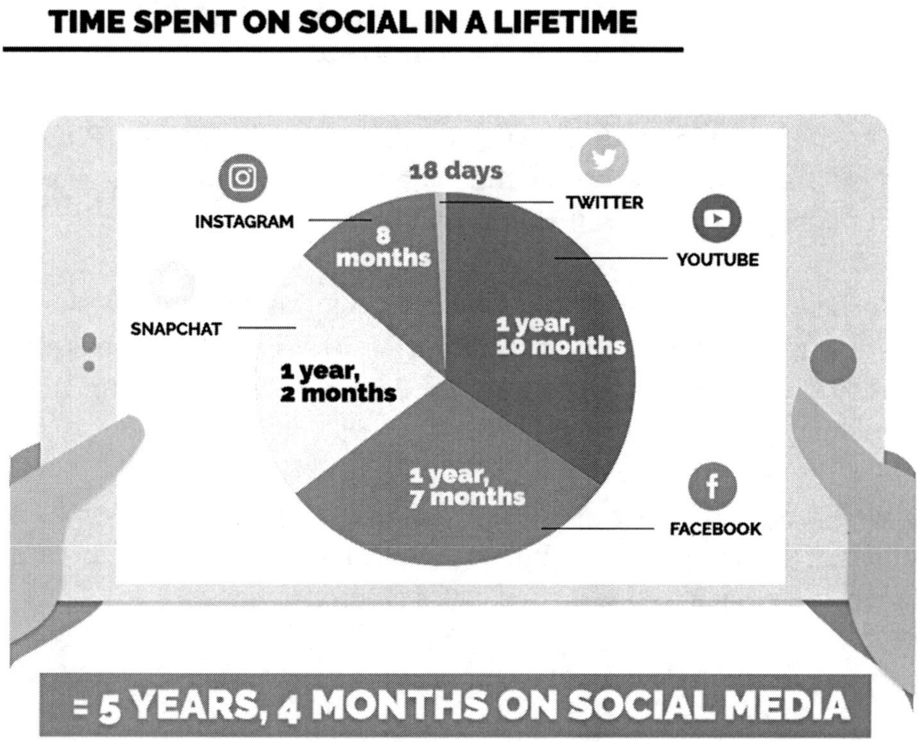

[Average Time Spent on Social Media in a Lifetime – Infographic by Mediakix]

What you do in your social media time is well known to you– "*mostly*" useless scrolling, watching random photos & videos, connecting with unknown people without any purpose, reading news which includes fake news & rumors as well, chatting, & most importantly "*stay connected*", right?

Few may justify it excusing that they read news & get updates on social media. Well, why don't you use some awesome news apps out there? Interestingly, these 2 hours doesn't include WhatsApp, TV, gaming time & time spent on other like activities, otherwise the number could be even bigger. But even if you save these 2 hours for some meaningful tasks like reading or skills building, you can add 2 hours to your 24 hours day. *After all,* ***an hour saved is an hour produced! This way you can make your day of 26 hours!***[13]

Further, as per 2018 *Internet Trends Report* by *Kleiner Perkins Caufield Byers*[14], average screen time of a typical U.S. adult has grown from 5.6 hours a day to 5.9 hours a day.

Social Media is growing all time (no declining trends). Facebook now has 220+ crore users, Pinterest has 20+ crore, Spotify has 17+ crore & Netflix has 12.5+ crore users! People now spend more time on mobile apps than watching TV[15].

Well, that's a little glimpse into the world of social media addiction & how much time it eats up! Next, we are going to discuss Why is social media so addictive. Let's go on...

6.3 Why Is Social Media So Addictive?

Well, social Media apps are designed to be addictive! *Julian Morgans* in a *VICE* article titled "*Your Addiction to Social Media Is No Accident*" rightly stated:

> *"Today, most of us reach for Snapchat, Instagram, Facebook, or Twitter with one vague thought in mind: Maybe someone liked my stuff.*[16]"

Social Media apps are designed after hijacking human minds! Take the messaging apps for example. When you chat with someone, you constantly see those three dots with "... is typing" & it lets you stay within the app to see what's coming in for you! Situation has become so worst that now people who created or helped create these platforms are quitting social media over addiction fears[17].

In disguise of engagement, social media platforms are selling your quality time to advertisers. The more time you waste on social media, the more these platforms earn. Your quality time is what you pay for earnings of the social media giants.

Your quality time is what you pay for earnings of the social media giants.

It will not be unfair to say that *you don't use social media, but social media use you to feed the greed of their founders/ creators and investors.* They are not worried about your mental health, but about their next financials.

I'm not sure, but I do think that the loading time of Facebook is no incidence, but the simple strategy to keep you stuck with the app. I always wonder: Does Facebook really don't have engineers to look after it's loading time? I mean, it loads content at such a slow pace. Twitter doesn't do that, Instagram doesn't do that, other platforms doesn't do that but Facebook. And yeah... I also think that Instagram can also do the same in some upcoming update. After all, Instagram is also enjoying the same leadership as Facebook does! Then, all we will get is just another apology from Facebook, citing it as a coding or other like issue! Very well managed!

Regarding WhatsApp: Yes, it also enjoys Facebook leadership, but I don't think it will follow that strategy as it is not in a unique position like Instagram & it has got its rivals.

Infinite scrolling feature in our social feeds, auto-play of next video & track, use of trigger colors, pull-to-refresh to discover something new & check for new updates, notification numbers – all of these are just few examples of how social media is designed to be addictive!

In social media design, either there are no "real ethics" or there are "minimal ones"! At times, I see all the social media networks as a game of psychology that their makers have mastered & in which all the community members are losers!

Our psychological vulnerabilities are exploited. Take YouTube for example. On YouTube, you go for a specific video, but how many times you stop at just that one? I think you got my point! Yep! YouTube auto-load feature is turned-on by default feeding you with next video once the current one is finished! Even if you turn-off the auto-load feature, once your current video is finished, you find your device screen filled with recommendations based on your interests & history! That recommendations are just hard to ignore, right? Well, for Google, it's just a better user-experience & that's okay! On another side, it's a feature that keep you hooked for hours on YouTube. My point is: Social Media is addictive, "*major by design*"! It's designed to be addictive.

Further, Social Media Addiction is a kinda chemical issue as well & the chemical, which is culprit here is "*Dopamine*". Let's know more about it...

Dopamine is the "Ultimate Culprit"

When you turn to social media, it gives you instant relief due to release of the brain chemical called "*dopamine*" (we'll not go into technical details here, alright? By the way, it's the same chemical release that rewards you for accomplishing a goal[18]). You can become attached to that feeling of relief & find yourself helpless to give your social media use a break & you want more of it! That feeling of relief is one of the major factors for social media addiction.

You get a new notification. Your phone rings! You don't know what's there in the notification. It's like a surprise for you! You want to reveal that surprise or notification right now & find yourself unable to stop doing it. You pick your phone, unlock it & check what's new! Sometimes it's a new mail from a marketing company, sometimes it's a Facebook Friend message asking "howdy", sometimes it's Instagram telling you that your post has got a new comment & so on! That's it!

How many notifications are really worth your time? I don't think even 10% do! Tech companies know how push notifications excites you[19] & that's why all of them seek your permission to land their newbies in your notification center! Every time you see a notification, it triggers brain neuro-chemical 'dopamine' which increases your curiosity & compel you to check the notification. After, checking notification, dopamine releases, which makes you feel good!

Every like, every notification, every retweet, every comment & share you get, your "*Dopamine Feeling*" gets a boost & you become addicted to that feeling. Now when you want to quit it, you simply find it hard[20].

6.4 Cure to Social Media Addiction

While it's true that social media apps are designed to be addictive, it's also true that how you use social media, is in your hands. As A. P. J. Abdul Kalam wrote in his book "*My Journey: Transforming Dreams into Actions*" –

> *"It is only when we are faced with failure do we realise that these resources were always there within us. We only need to find them and move on with our lives." – A. P. J. Abdul Kalam*

Resources you need to do anything, are always within you. Well, that's a philosophical take, but useful & implementable.

Though there is no hard & fast trick, or a dedicated rehab center for Social Media Addiction Treatment, but there are little things that can have big impact in shaping your social media habits in positive ways. We'll discuss them in later sections of this book.

Before proceeding further, I want to clarify one very important thing related to Social Media Addiction. You might be thinking that 'Addiction" is too harsh word for social media. Why don't I use the word "obsession"? Well, I got your concern. You don't want to call yourself an addict. May be, you are not an addict. Perhaps obsession is the case for you. Well, for that, we need to understand the difference between Social Media Obsession & Social Media Addiction. Let's explore more about it...

6.5 Social Media Obsession versus Social Media Addiction

Let's Draw the "Thick" Line between Social media Obsession & Social Media Addiction

I believe that these days the term "Social Media Addiction" is overused. Many people are not "addicted" to social media, they are just "obsessed"! To understand the difference between the two, we need to draw a "***thick***" line and that thick line is "**control**"!

Yes! The main difference between "*Social Media Addiction*" & "*Social Media Obsession*" is control.

As long as you are able to control your social media behavior, you are not an addict, no matter for how much time you are using social media.

If you feel compelled to use social media & find yourself unable to stop using it, you are an addict, no matter for how much time, for how many times, when, where and how you are using it.

Control is the only thing that makes the difference. We can also call it by other names like self-discipline, but the substance of all such things point to just one thing: **control**!

I do think that today, most people have the compulsion of using social media. So, throughout this book, I will be using the term "*Social Media Addiction*" & not "*Social Media Obsession*".

-Let's Do One Experiment-

If you want to find out whether you're an addict or obsessed, just do one little experiment on yourself. It's simple & demands no cost except your courage & determination. So, are you ready? I hope you said yes & with that hope, let me tell you about that experiment:

"A day without social media"

Yes, that's the experiment. Try to spend a day without using any social media service.

If you get through this, it's a great sign that you're not an addict & you can control your social media. If you fail, don't worry. I've got lots of tricks & tips for you in subsequent sections of Calm Social Media. Those will help you surely. So, just relax!

As of now, we'll discuss the next issue of Social Media Abuse & that one is: "Use of Social Media by or for Underaged or Small Children. Let's go for it...

7.0 Use of Social Media by or for Underaged or Small Children

7.1 Age is Not Just A Number!

Age! I don't believe the saying "*Age is just a number*" because I believe that "*Age is **not** just a number*".

With age, one learns many things in life. Our intellect develops with age. There is legal age for marriage, for drinking, for becoming a prime minister, for becoming a president, for retirement, for becoming a judge, for becoming a Chartered Accountant & the list goes on & on! Fortunately, there is legal age for using certain social media & internet services by children as well...

... Children's Online Privacy Protection Act[21] ("COPPA") is there to protect the privacy & internet safety of children who are under 13 years of age. Most of the social media services are available to people who are over 13 years of age. Well, that's law...

... Having law in place is one thing & it's proper implementation is another thing. We have the former but not the latter in place. Want to know reason behind it?...

... Well, internet kids are smart enough to manipulate their online birth date, skip the age wall & get their profiles active on platforms they want! Today, anybody with an internet device can create an email-ID with any date of birth. Kids are not fools! They know it very well what date of birth they should use to enter the services meant for older people. That's just one aspect of this 13-year-age loophole! Don't worry about it. I thought about this issue & one solution came to my mind. I will discuss it with you later. As of now, just focus on the issue of Underaged using social media...

7.2 What Parents Are Doing?

In the current era, I have seen so-called "*modern parents*" are creating profiles for their kids and toddlers. What an urgency! Isn't it? Before child even grow up enough to fulfil the legal age required to create a social profile, their profiles are built by their parents. That's what I have seen. Let's talk some data now...

As per recent studies, the average age of child for getting a phone has fallen to 10. There are instances where children of the age as low as 3 have dedicated smartphones. Too much smartphone & social media is neither good nor smart for our children. Net effect is that it makes them feel sad, lonely, depressed & at worst, suicidal[22].

Research found that 1 in 4 children under 6 years of age have their own smartphones[23]. Most surprising finding is that about 50% of such children spend about 3 hours per day glued to their smartphone. 11 is the age which is considered suitable to "deserve" a smartphone but here we are: 25% parents buying smartphones for their "so little babies"!

I don't think it's a right move since 6 or less is not the age where one can understand things like internet connected smartphones & social media. It can open a world for children which is not suitable for them (consider social media bullying for example).

Some people can argue that they are using parental control. Well, any parental control can't reduce the smartphone risk to zero! And what's the point of handing over a dedicated phone to a kid of such age? For children of age 2-5 years, recommended screen time is 1 hour maximum[24] & that too under parental supervision.

Children under 13[25] years of age need strict supervision for their online safety. There are specific regulations like "*COPPA*" as well dedicated to children under 13 years of age for their protection in the online world. COPPA requires online service providers to get parental consent before collecting personal information of children. Why is such regulation in place? Think about it! Got it? So, do you still want to hand over a smartphone to your kid? I think no. With that hope, let's proceed further...

7.3 "Sharenting" – Problem of "Social Media Sharing + Parenting"

A new trend called "***Sharenting***" (a combination of "share" & "parenting") is also there.

Some parents are keen to share their kids' photos (including inappropriate ones), private & embarrassing information (including location) on social media, which can pose risks to a child's privacy.[26] Neither you can ask for a toddler's permission, nor s/he is in a situation to grant it! What you share about your kids can embarrass them when they grow up.

As per survey, more than 1 in 4 children feel embarrassed, anxious & worried for their pictures posted by their parents.[27] Is it a good idea making our children's life public? I think no.

With no offence & without any intention of hurting anybody's sentiments, I would like to firmly say this: parents need to understand that when children grow up, they have their own choices, their own circles & groups, their own preferences. Posting their childhood photos on social media may be a cool thing for you, but not for your grown-up child. Some may find it offensive as well.

Further, very small kids are not able to talk or speak their emotions, but when they grow up, their childhood posts can be a thing of public mockery! They may feel bad!

I understand that childhood memories are precious, but I also feel that making them public is not a good choice. It's better that relation between children & parents remains real & personal. Why make it virtual & public? Sharenting can do some good only in short-run, like making you happy when you share something about your kid, get advice on parental matters, but given its negative outcomes like threat to children's security & privacy, it can hurt a care free childhood in the long-run.

I would like to appeal you to stop sharenting, if you do! Also ask people around you to do the same! It can do a lot of good to our children.

Final choice lies on you, of course. I am nobody to tell you anything. I am just saying what I believe, and I am sharing my belief with you because I feel that this thought can change the perspective of parents & guardians reading this book & it can bring a positive change in the life of their children & resultantly in their own life as well.

7.4 Messenger Kids - Facebook Danger Extended to Kids

Surprisingly Facebook has targeted kids aged 6+ with its app "*Messenger Kids*"![28] At the age of 6, how much understanding one can have? Does a 6-year-old kid really need his/her own messenger account? I don' think so. A kid at 6 is just not ready to deal with all such stuff.

I think "Messenger Kids" is simply an example of Facebook's greed to grow its platform at any cost. Any person with some sensitivity to children will oppose such kind of apps. Anything that is legal doesn't mean that it's healthy as well...

... Take alcohol for example. If you are 18/21/25 years old (drinking age varies under global laws), you can drink a bottle of it! There is no legal ban on it. But is it healthy? Of course not. If you really love someone or care about someone, you don't want him/her to drink a bottle of alcohol even though it's legal, because you know that it's not good for health...

... Same goes for *Messenger Kids*. The argument that *Messenger Kids* complies with all legal requirements, is the most foolish argument anybody can give to support the app. These people are not considering the psychological & health impact of it![29] People behind these services know very well how addictive their services are! Does Facebook want our kids to spend hours on messenger instead of playground or schools? Such apps can become their new pastime killing their spare time & creativity...

... I would like to also mention that each habit is developed by choice. Initially parents have the choice whether to opt for *Messenger kids* for their children. If they opt for it & the kids become addictive to the app (which can be the case given the addictive nature of the service), it can ruin their children. They will not be able to focus on their studies, sports or anything even in their childhood days. It can take away their Carefree World away from them. To sum it up, I think *Messenger Kids* is one of the most harmful gifts from Facebook to our kids!

7.5 What Are Kids up to?

Children play online games, watch videos on Netflix & YouTube for hours, cutting physical sports activities & sleep (which are an essential part of a healthy childhood)! Two of the best examples of how social media & smartphones are destroying kids childhood are

YouTube videos & games like *Candy Crush* (children have more crush on this game than anything else!).

You might have come across children as young as just 3 years old playing alone with their smartphone. Is it safe for them? I mean, these smartphones are connected to internet, have all type of notifications & all type of content. Just a wrong word typed on Google can open a lot of content inappropriate for kids. To stop this, it's important that we keep a watch on what type of games our kids are playing, what videos they are watching, what they are googling and what they are reading!

As I was writing this, I remember one incident related to this issue. I want to share it with you...

... My 5-years old niece visited home recently & he came across one of my old phones (Windows 10 Phone which I don't use now). I didn't stop him as that phone was unused for quite a while & didn't have any games or YouTube installed...

... To my surprise, he was able to connect the phone to Wi-Fi, install some games from the Windows Store & watching videos on YouTube in the Microsoft Edge! When I caught all this, I was shocked! I mean, today a 5-year-old kid knows how to operate all this, right? Well, I don't see anything wrong in this. I am just worried about negative aspects of kids knowing all this stuff! For this, let me share the second incident...

... The second incident happened in Metro! I was out for some office work, travelling in metro without catching a seat (as we are mostly seated in office, right?) & reading some tax documents. I was focused on going through the documents as I had limited time & I need to finish all the stuff before reaching the Income Tax Department! A lady was travelling with her crying baby (who, I think was 3-5 years in age). Well, I didn't bother as crying is a usual thing for babies 😊 ...

... In a few moments, my focus was halted. I realized, that lady had started playing some Hindi songs on YouTube (& that too in a high volume!) to put her baby in calm mode! I remained silent for the sake of the baby! I just put the documents in my bag & started looking at what's the baby was doing with the phone (though I am not a spy or any person who intrude or invade people's private space, but I do observe people's public activities, which I think can be quoted in my work like Calm Social Media) ...

... After few moments, the lady went in lite-sleep mode & the kid was alone with the smartphone. The current song finished & next started playing (thanks to YouTube's auto-play!). Well, the next video was just inappropriate for that kid & I was about to stop that in a moment. Before, I could do that, one senior gentleman, sitting next to the baby's seat took hold of the matter. He took the phone from the baby, closed YouTube & woke-up the lady with a loud & angry "*excuse me*". He told the lady what's going on & scold her as well to teach her a lesson on child-care, parenting & online safety ...

... I was glad to see that at least some people do care about these issues. Anyway, that's the exact thing I want to tell you. Kids with "*smartphones-with-no-supervision*" is a very dangerous thing & can do irreversible harm to their life. So, be aware. Take the responsibility of protecting them from all kinds of online abuse. Sit with them when they are using smartphones or similar kind of devices. It's worth your time.

Further, it's no secret that more screen time is directly linked with unhappiness[30]. Kids spending more time on video games, social media, chatting & other online activities are less happy than kids spending time in physical activities. So, if you want your kids to be happy, cut their screen time & involve them in activities like sports, reading, meeting with real people or just let them carry on some other recreational activities like painting (kids love it), playing some musical instruments, et cetera!

That's all for this section. I've got a lot more to say about social media, smartphones & parenting. Will do that with subsequent related issues. For now, let's discuss one of the most common Social Media Abuse Issue – FOMO i.e. Fear of Missing Out...

8.0 FOMO: Fear of Missing Out

8.1 FOMO: General Perspective

What is "*Fear of Missing Out*" or "*FOMO*"? I think its name says it all. Anyway, let's know about it!

To keep it simple, FOMO[31] is the "*fear or a situation in which you feel that if you're not online or not active on social media, you may be missing on to what's going on*".

FOMO creates a pressure & anxiety forcing you to "*stay online*" so that you don't feel missed out. If you're "*disconnected*" even for a short duration, FOMO can cause lots of anxiety & loneliness for you!

Want to know more about it? Okay! Don' use Facebook for a couple of days & lose the track of your friends' activity. On doing that, if you are feeling more & more compelled to check Facebook & know about them, what are they doing, that's a kinda "*FOMO feeling*".

It's a psychological issue & obviously, does not add anything positive to your life. People "*high on FOMO*"[32], frequently check their phones even in the situations where they are not supposed to do so, like when driving or attending lectures, studying, et cetera. These things show that FOMO has potential to cause lots of damage to your life. It's better be cured, right?

8.2 FOMO Reality

"*Lots of people*" check their Facebook, Twitter & "*What's New*" even before leaving their bed in the morning. What's that? I guess FOMO & the no-brainer desire to be on top of "*everything*".

To me, "*Fear of Missing Out*" or "*FOMO*" is just an excuse to justify one's addiction to social media. Someone has rightly said:

> *"We shouldn't be afraid of missing out on what's going on in the social media world, but of what we could be missing by spending too much time in it"*

You keep your eye on all your social media profiles out there claiming that you need to know what's going on.

Well, just stop peeping into others' lives. If you want updates, get some sensible ones. There are lots of awesome news & knowledge apps[33]. Grab some for you. It will make you more knowledgeable, skilled, confident & fulfilled. You will know what the world is up-to instead of getting fake news & knowing what your friends or "*Just friend*" is up-to. You know what I mean, right?

8.3 Life Without Online Friends: My Experiment

Life is much better without online friends. I know that you will not trust this claim of mine so easily! No worries. Let me share my personal experience with you. I think that will make you change your mind...

... It's been about 2 years since I decided to reduce my Facebook friends' list to zero. In September 2017, I disabled the Facebook app as well. No more messages, notifications & scrolling & the experience I enjoy is rare (because not many people *dare to delete Facebook*) as well as relaxing. I never looked back since then (except some testing & few experimental chats for writing this book) ...

You might be thinking about what my Facebook friends thought of me? Well, I called the ones who really care about me & whom I care about. I let them know what I was doing & they felt happy for me. A few also told me that they would try it too "*someday*" ...

The free phone space I got by deleting the app (about 400 MB) was used to download some sensible apps like The Guardian, Flipboard, Business Insider, Google Primer among others...

... The time wasted on chats & scrolling was used in reading & taking notes in OneNote & Evernote (Yes, I use both of them for different purpose). I purchased more books & start finishing them at a faster pace! More time was devoted to my goals. I was happier than ever & self-proclaimed most productive person at work...

... No status updates from anybody! No more notifications for who liked what or who shared what or whom should I wish today! It's a very good feeling...

... You must give it a try. Just try deleting Facebook! You don't need Facebook to stay in touch with people you really care about. Why don't plan a visit or simply pick the phone to have a call. That's more satisfying & personal.

Delete Facebook & like apps. Connect real, not virtual. No e-chat can replace real chat, right? Do it & feel the difference.

And yeah... don't worry about news or things you care about. There are much better apps for it. You will not be missing out. Instead, you will have a good time. You'll learn much more than Social Media News Feeders & you'll be smarter! That's my promise.

9.0 Negative Health Caused by Social Media

Let's explore how social media is taking health & well-being away from you & awarding you with unwanted gifts like blindness, stress, sleep deprivation, anxiety, depression, unhappiness & negativity

9.1 Making People Blind – Literally & Healthily

Smartphone & social media has made people blind & for few, the statement is true in its literal sense! There have been cases where people has lost their eyesight due to their smartphone, social media & gaming addiction...

... A 21-yeat old Chinese woman lost her eyes partially after playing a game called "*Honour of Kings*" for a continuous period of 24 hours. She used to play that game regularly for 8 hours[34]!

Well, that's one of the extreme cases of how badly Social Media Abuse can affect your health. Apart from your eyes, social media, screen time & so-called fun-games impact your health in many negative ways like depression & other mental-health disorders, sleep-cuts & sleep-deprivation, to name a few. Excessive time spent on social media also results in loss of time for real socializing, exercise & other recreational activities which also add to the "*minus health points of social media*".

You can't use social media '*in air without eyes*'! Apart from time, social media leads to excessive use of your eyes, neck, back and the ultimate body. Your Social Media Addiction has a major role to play in severe health problems.

-Once Small Tip for Your Eye-Care-

When your eyes are constantly glued to screen, it negatively impacts the eye's vision-power and can lead to severe eye related issues. Though you can't avoid the gadgets (since we are living in a 21st century online world!), but you can use one small tip to help your eyes.

Just looking away from the screen for at least 20 seconds after each 20-minute screen time can do a lot of good to your eyes. So, look away from your screen every 20 minutes![35] I am not saying that it needs to be exact 20 minutes. You got it, right?

9.2 Sleep Deprivation

Scrolling through your smartphone screen in bed at night is a ritual, right? Yep! It should not be like this. Blue light emitting from screen & the interactive nature of gadgets is overstimulating & can excite your mood.

While you should be in calm mode at night, the stimulation created by your phone can cost your sleep. Research suggests that people who spend more time on social media are more likely to suffer from sleep disturbances.[36]

A study of 1 million U.S. teens found that teens who spent more time on the internet, playing computer games, social media, texting, using video chat or watching TV were less happy than those who spent more time seeing their friends in person, exercising, playing sports, attending religious services, reading, or even doing homework[37]...

... The study concluded: Activities that doesn't include screen time leads to more happiness than activities that include screen time. While the study involved only teens, I believe that its results can be applied to people in all age-groups.

9.3 Building Stress, Depression & Suicidal Thoughts

Social Media & smartphones are "*rich source of stress, depression & building suicidal thoughts*". I know you won't believe me. No worries. To support this claim, I would like to quote an excerpt from

FastCompnay.com article, (*interestingly*) titled "*Maybe It's Time To Regulate Gadgets And Apps Like Cigarettes*[38]". Here we go:

> *"those who spent more than three hours a day on a mobile device were 34% more likely to suffer "suicide-related outcome" than kids who used them two hours a day or less. Another finding showed that kids who used social media every day were 13% more likely to report feelings of depression."*

Further study found that frequent users of social media have 2.7 times higher chances of developing depression. To make the situation worst, it was also found that people with depression symptoms turn to social media more often as perhaps they find it hard to engage themselves in direct social relationships.[39]

It's a kind of "*Social Media Trap*", as the more time you spend on social media, more are the chances of depression, which again leads to more time spend on social media!

It suggests that the less time you spend on social media, the better. Again, I would like to add here that social media brings many good things to your life, it's just Social Media Abuse which is the cause of the problem. I hope you get me right!

Now you know that social media causes depression & stress. Don't you also want to know the reasons for it? Well, I think one of the biggest reasons for this is "*Fake Happiness*" of others! Yep! Fake Happiness.

On social media, everybody seems to be happy. Each time you land in your feed, you see people sharing their vacation photos, pics with their brand-new cars, travelling in planes, smiling selfies with some awesome background places, & you can add hundreds of thousands of scenarios to the list. And guess what? When you are looking at those photos, you are sitting in your home or in the cubicle of your office!...

... You don't even know if these "*Social People*" are genuinely happy or not, but you certainly feel that they are happier than you. To change this mindset of yours, you need to make it clear that on social media, all people posts only good moments from their life. That can make you feel that their life is better than yours while this may not be the case!

"Anybody's social wall doesn't give a true picture of their life. It's highly manipulated!"

You can't know what's going on in one's life just by having a look into their social profiles.

Much of the Social Media World is much-much far away from much of the Real World.

When you are trapped in the illusion created by such fake world, you find yourself less worthy & raise questions on your achievements. It's simple comparison, frequently (or "technically") termed as "Peer Pressure" as well!...

... Oh! I just used the term "Peer Pressure". I have to say a lot about it but will do it later. As of now, let's focus on other health issues caused by social media...

9.4 Social Media's Narcissism: Unearned Self-Importance

Social Media is so stressful that instead of 8 hours of standard sleep, now you need 8.5 hours of sleep to compensate for the increased stress. It also impacts your memory and ability to think. Indulging in just yourself on social media like posting excessive selfies, your plan for the day or vacation, sharing your thoughts & opinions on everything & anything and then feeling a need for admiration on whatever you post can lead to the situation of "*narcissism*" - a disorder in which a person has an inflated sense of self-importance.[40]

To me, Calm Social Media seems to be a perfect solution for at least Social Media's Narcissism. So, don't worry about it. As we proceed further, you'll find lots of tips & tricks to Calm Social Media. Just keep reading...

9.5 Yes! Social Media Makes You Unhappy

Speaking mathematically, unhappiness & social media are directly proportional! Increased technology use is linked to increased depression & unhappiness. *The Atlantic* reported:

> *"recent research suggests that screen time, in particular social-media use, does indeed cause unhappiness.*[41]*"*

People who meet their friends in person are happier than those who connect with them online.

Study found that students spending time on internet, online games & social media are less happy.

"Social Media & happiness are inversely proportional"

It can be inferred that "*Non-Screen Time = Happiness*" & "*Screen Time = Unhappiness*". Yeah... you may argue that you feel happy when you play candy crush or when you chat on Facebook & WhatsApp. Well, that happiness is temporary...

... As soon as you turn off your phone or desktop, you feel craving to go back to gaming or Facebook & WhatsApp, but you just can't do it 24/7 and you feel unhappy for not getting what you want?

The more you use social media like Facebook, Twitter, Instagram, WhatsApp, more are chances of you being unhappy & negative. Use of social media add stress, increase anxiety & can disturb your sleep as well since you keep on "*Scrolling not Sleeping*".

Quitting Social Media is better option as this action will improve your well-being & keep you happy in the *long-run*.[42]

9.6 Social Media Making You Feel Guilty

You know yourself better than anyone else (don't trust anybody who says s/he know you better than you do yourself! It's nothing but non-sense, really). You start scrolling through the social media (mind-boggling!) wall... you lost in the social media world... when you come back in real world... you realize that hours have passed by since you start scrolling! Time that could be used in doing some meaningful stuff has gone. Time you waste on social media leaves you with a feeling of guilt in your mind that you wasted your time.

9.7 Surprising Facebook Experiment About Your Happiness

In an experiment, people were asked to give up their Facebook account for a week. The result was shocking. After weekend, they felt happier than those who used their accounts.

The more time you spend on Facebook, the more are the chances of having symptoms of depression & feeling lonely.

It was also found that your screen time is the reason for unhappiness, your unhappiness is not the reason for screen time[43].

Shocked? Well, that's what study found! Anyway, let's move on to the very next & very interesting issue: Peer Pressure...

10.0 Peer Pressure & Inferiority Complex

10.1 What's Peer Pressure?

We can call it "*comparison*" in simple language. In the world of social media, *Peer Pressure* can be understood as the stress or pressure to match yourself with activities & status of other people, when you compare yourself with others on social media. Social media, with your permission, offers new opportunities to you for experiencing peer pressure every single day! Want an example? Okay! Here it is:

Your friend is on vacation & you are working on a serious project in your office! How does that feel? Don't you feel jealous and an urge to go there? You also want to post vacation photos. That's peer pressure. But you don't think the same way when you are on vacation and your friend is seeing your vacation photos on your Facebook and Instagram profile in his/her cubicle!

Because your friends, colleagues, neighbors, "*online friends*", (or name any member of your so-called "*Social Circle*") are doing it, you want to do it! Because they have it, you want to have it! That's peer pressure. It's nothing but result of no-brainer thinking. Think about it!

Some people compare their followers with followers of others, some compare their clothes, some compare their post likes with likes on others' post, some compare how many tweets they send a day & how many tweets their friends send a day or who is more active, some compare the places of vacation (my friend went on foreign vacation, I will also go on foreign vacation, cancel domestic bookings), some compare cars (my friend just purchased a brand new & I am driving my old one - not fair, need to get new one), and the list of comparison goes on & on...

Everybody's posting some great photos on their profile, no matter how much happy s/he is in real life. You just have a look at those photos and feel they are happy & you are not. You tend to show the world that you are happier and tend to post great (& sometimes fake; just saying!) photos on your profile, right?

10.2 How Peer Pressure Can Create Inferiority Complex?

Social Media is more of a fake world & less of a real world. On social media, leaving few exceptions aside, everybody is happy, there are no problems in anybody's life, everybody's career is thriving & life is fun & perfect. You can be overwhelmed by the "*social media perfect life*" of other people & when you compare your life & accomplishments with such high levels (though you don't even know if those are real), it can make you lose your confidence, you may feel of yourself unaccomplished & inferior to others and become a victim of inferiority complex.

10.3 Cure to Peer Pressure

Peer Pressure is the result of pointless comparison, foolish thinking in the mix world of reality & fakeness. If you feel Peer Pressure, it's just because you have lost your identity in this all-time-active world. You have forgotten how special you are, how unique you are. You have forgotten how unique your fingerprints are – nobody can match your fingerprints & you can't match fingerprints of others. Then why should you try to match other's status? Why don't you create a status of your own? Won't be it a better approach? I think it will be & a limitless one.

To put this solution in more simple terms: "*Just don't compare*"! My principle is simple: "*Compare you with you & be better than yourself*". With this approach, you don't set benchmark for yourself based on other's achievement or happiness level.

"Compare you with you & be better than yourself"

When you try to be better than you, the possibilities are endless & most importantly, the confidence is sky-rocketed! If you feel embarrassed from yourself, how can you expect others to respect you? First learn to respect yourself. Make firm decisions & be confident. Let me give you an example here from my own life (It's Snapchat related) ...

... Personally, I never used Snapchat. I just joined it to learn about it & because it's part of the process of my brands' marketing on social media. I was never active on the platform...

... One fine day, I was in one of my CA Final classes. One folk came to me & ask for my notebook (yeah... I was quite good at academics!). He was copying notes & in the meantime, he asked me for my Snap ID. I said I am not using Snapchat! He laughed. Well, I laughed in return...

... He was "*just another person*" who felt I'm tech-disabled person. Since, I was aware of the platform & the decision of not to use it was mine, I was confident in my answer. But even if I had not known about it, I would not be ridiculed since I know how to deal with those cunning smiles & laughs. The more aware you are, the better, but you don't need to know everything & nobody has the right to ridicule you...

... Anyway, back to that incidence, I didn't take it well. I showed him my website & let myself show off my tech skills to him! He got it! Well, my point here is not to ridicule anybody, but to make it clear that we need to be confident of who we are, what we do & what our choices are. We need to be strong enough so that nobody can force anything on us. I have seen people joining social media because of peer pressure, indulge in drinking & smoking because of peer pressure, going on bunk because of peer pressure & so on! If somebody would force me to smoke or drink, I would throw that guy away. Not to smoke/ drink is my decision & I know it's right for me. Nobody can change it...

... Same goes for social media. What social media network you should use, should be your own decision. if you are a kid/ teen, your parents/ guardian may guide you. There is no harm in that. Even if we are adults, there is no harm in seeking or accepting advice from our parents, "*true friends*" & people who really care about us...

... In any case, you shouldn't be a puppet of your so called "*social circle*". You must remember that those who create path for themselves & others are leaders. Those who just follow the path already created are followers. You choose yourself who you want to be.

11.0 Information Overload, Unfocused Life & Short Attention Span

Social media feeds are endless. It has news, updates from your friends, updates on topics, people & brands you are following & many other things impossible to list here! Your mind is always hungry for exploring something new! What's the solution you get: just start exploring what's new in the feed, right? That's where problem lies...

Average students focus only for 3 minutes while studying. Major distraction is from phone and social media. Few students check Facebook every 15 minutes[44]. It's really alarming. It is making people worst in their academic as well as professional life as they are simply not able to focus on their studies & work!

You are reading all type of content, whether or not its meaningful & relevant for you. When it comes to our news feed, we tend to forget what field we are in or what we do & who we are! For example, a doctor may not need to know what new immigration policy our President or Prime Minister has announced, but if it's there in the feed served with some catchy headline, he may read it, wasting his/her time on information s/he doesn't really need! That's just one aspect of information overload.

Gone are the days when you used to rely on just one morning newspaper! Today, mindless surfing, frequently checking news feeds on various social media networks is giving you information that neither you need, nor you can handle or remember. This over-information is making you unfocused & leaves you craving for something new every now & then. This craziness to be on the top of "*What's happening*" has left with short attention span, which can be as short as 3 minutes!

-One Interesting Solution for Students: An Inspiration-

Interestingly, few people are coming up with innovative solutions to tackle the problem of Social Media Abuse. Here, I would like to discuss about an app called "*Hold*[45]" which, as of now, is available only for UK University students to deal with their smartphone addiction.

Invented by "*Maths Mathisen*", *Hold* app pays students for not using their smartphone! All they have to do is just don't look at their phone for a continues 20 minutes time (really hard task! Isn't it?) and they will get a point that can be used to order a pizza or grab discount on Amazon shopping. App also has plans to expand to other educational & work areas in future (I hope its expansion for general public as well).

Well, it's kinda of bribe to those who are slaves of their phones (no offence)! I think it's a great idea to save students from modern slavery.

12.0 Social Media Bullying & Harassment

12.1 What Is It?

I'm "*quite*" sure that you've heard of cyberbullying! Anyway, I'm not assuming anything. So, let's discuss it.

Cyberbullying[46], which is also called "cyber-harassment" or "cyberstalking", means use of technology, social media and other digital & electronic media to harass, mistreat, embarrass, threaten and bully someone in the online world.

Social Media bullying & harassment is one of the most common types of cyberbullying, especially among teens & kids.

Social Media Bullying has become a common thing on social media platforms like Facebook, Instagram, Snapchat & Twitter[47]. Few examples include sending threating messages, posting false, personal or negative information about someone, posting personal photos & videos without asking for permission of the concerned person, et cetera.

Worst part of online bullying is that, due to its online nature, it happens 24/7 because bully as well as bullied are connected all time on the internet & social media. In case, no report/ action is taken against it, there is no relief to the person who is bullied, as long as s/he has internet access. Also, children are hesitant to talk about this, so it's hard to notice for parents and as well as teachers & others!

12.2 Cyberbullying Stats, Impact & Consequences

Exact cyberbullying stats can't be determined as many people don't report about it. However, as per study, about 1 in 4 teens has faced cyberbullying. 25% is a huge number! Further, about 1 in 6 teens has admit that they had cyberbullied someone.[48] These stats make it clear what our children are facing & what our children are doing! There is no doubt that lots of them are not on the right path & we have got a job to do.

As per one survey, 82% of children in age group of 5-7 years, 96% of children in age group of 8-11 years & 99% of children in the age group of 12-15 years, are using social media![49] We well know the understanding level of children of such age. They are simply vulnerable.

More than 82% of online sex crime is originating from social media. The number of such cases has doubled in the last 3 years & 75% of the victims are girls! Shocking part is that only 1 in 5 cases is reported to legal authorities. Means in 80% of the cases, the bullies are freely enjoying their lives. The crime doesn't stop here...

... You will be surprised to know that 90% of children in the age-group of 8-16 years have seen pornography. 90%![50] Sometimes it's intentional, while at other times it's unintentional and a part of cyber-crime where children are forced to watch pornography!...

... It's shameful. We live in so-called civilized society. Is this the civilization we want to gift our children? I don't think we have reached a level to call ourselves civilized. What kind of civilized society is this where our children are exposed to such kind of things. They are exposed to bullying, threatening, suicides, forced pornography & what's not! And still, some people think that if 5-year old child is on social media, it's modernity, it's cool. I think these dumb people needs to be taught & I'm not sorry for my words here. Children are the future & they deserve a Carefree childhood. If they are subjected such brutal crimes, we all can predict what kind of future we will have. The trend shows how drastically the problem is rising. Sadly, our children are the victims of all this inhumanity.

As per Australian research[51], nearly 50% of the women in the online world have faced harassment & cyberbullying including threats of rape, sexual harassment, death & physical violence. 76% of those are under 30.

Such harassment and abuse cause negativity & result in depression. My take on this is simple (& it's not only for women but for men as well. You may take it, leave it, or hate it. It's up-to you.): *stop talking to random guys*! There is no need of "*being in touch*" with the world. To support my advice further, I would like to tell you that including strangers in your social network can negatively impact your self-esteem as well.[52]

No wonder, bullying (whether online or offline) does no good to anyone. Social Media Bullying is not limited to schools, streets or any other particular place. It's in the phone, tablet, desktop. As long as our children are online, they are exposed to online bullying...

... Bullying leads to bad reputation for each person involved which can have a negative impact on their career as well as personal life. It also causes depression, anxiety, suicidal thoughts & other mental health issues. At worst, bullies as well as bullied involve themselves in suicide attempts & unfortunately, some attempts have been successful[53] in the past (which is 2nd ranked cause of death for individuals in the age group of 15-24 years[54]). It's very sad & enough to conclude that cyberbullying is not a lite issue.

It also has legal consequences. There are different anti-bullying laws in different countries to deal with bullying of various kinds including cyberbullying. Let me tell you that cyberbullying is a crime with severe repercussions. Bullies can be sued & the convict can be imprisoned for as long as 10 years depending on the case (this is as per U.S. Federal Law[55]. Different countries have different laws in place).

I hope that you're not involved in any bullying activities. If unfortunately, you are, take care of the morality & humanity, treat people with respect & dignity, and take corrective actions, else law will take its course & convict can be behind bars (I hope you get me right!).

If you are a victim, don't worry. Law is with you! Moral people (who are more powerful than evil people) are with you. Just speak about this to your loved ones. Don't limit it to yourself. Once you talk about it to those who care about you, you'll feel relieved & more secure. No matter what's your age, just give it a talk. People of all ages need support. And one more thing... while talking about this, feel confident & don't be nervous as bully is at fault, not you.

12.3 What You Can Do?

I have felt the general & typical perception of "*most*" people about bullying. They feel that the people who are bullied are weak, have some shortcomings of their own or are just not strong enough to deal with the situation. Well, I never thought like that & I'm glad that I found this psychological opinion or advice or suggestion (I don't know what to call it, exactly) to support my opinion:

> *"bullying is not about you, or some flaw of yours. It's about the bully's need to control" - Jenise Harmon, Psychotherapist at Psych Central*[56]

First of all, we need to understand one thing – bullying is the consequence of insecurities of bullies & their vicious desire to feel empowered. So, if I'm bullied or you're bullied, or any other person is bullied or harassed at any point in life, it's not because of our fault, it's because of the fault of the bullies. Bullies are weak, not us. Bullies should be punished, not us. Bullies' life should be hell, not ours. So, don't even think to harm yourself. We're human beings – the most intelligent creature of the nature. We can overcome any situation. Yes, any situation &, bullying is no different.

I have heard it many times, I have said it many times & I will say it again: *there is always a long way to go...*

So, always think long-term. Okay? Yep! I hope you're feeling stronger now. Let's discover more about cyberbullying to have a deeper understanding & get ourselves ready to fight against it...

Cyberbullying is a major issue with kids & teens, so as a parent you need to keep an eye on your children's online health. There are lots of predators hunting on the internet & social media. For those who don't know about online predator, *it's a person, or I can say a bad person, who communicate with children over internet to commit child sexual abuse...*

... Social Media has enabled such bad people to make contact with children, chat with them online, make connections with them, & later on, force them into illegal sensual activities. Today, unregulated social media use of children, coupled with online predators, have made social media a facilitator of child abuse. It's a very serious matter & the biggest responsibility lies on the parents or guardian of the children. Internet is expanding & so the number of online predators.

If you find out that any child is bullied or is involved in bullying activities, ***don't scold*** him/her. Since they are not responsible for what happened. They are just too young to understand all this. Let them know that they are not alone & they have not done anything wrong. Once you have their confidence, next part is how to ***take their minds away from what happened*** & how to protect them from involving in such activities in future...

... I think you as parent/ guardian, know that well. We all have our own way of taking care of the children (but please be polite with them. I request). So, I'm not going to discuss all that stuff here. If you want me to go into that, please let me know about it along with your suggestions. I will do a post on it & will also include that in the next edition of this book.

Even though I am not capable of delivering a lesson on parenting, I would still like to discuss some important things to help you with *Social Media & Parenting*. Some of them are here, while others will be discussed in subsequent sections:

Don't allot a separate device to your underage child. Let them use yours. If you want to allot a separate device, use parental control tools & apps. You can find a good list of them on the web. Block the sites that may be harmful for your children. And yes, you don't have to do it manually. Just grab a tool for it. There are plenty of options available. Again, find it on the web. This way you can keep internet safe for your child.

Further, instead of laptop & a portable device, it would be better if you ***get a desktop*** and install it in an ***open space*** in your home. It will put a ***moral check*** on your child. Also, occasionally, keep looking for what they search, what they watch, what they listen & whom they contact online. You may also have your own control measures. Feel free to share your tips with me. Will combine them all in ever-updated post on Calm Social Media Blog & will also include those in the next edition of this book.

Now we have discussed Social Media Bullying & Harassment. Let's move on to the next issue of Social Media Abuse – Lost Creativity & Intelligence...

13.0 Lost Creativity & Intelligence

If you think that your 24/7 access to phone, internet & all-time connectivity on social media makes you smart, you are wrong. The fact is that smartphone & social media is fooling you in many ways & reducing your intelligence as well as creativity...

... Video games, internet, Social media and other such things in your phone impact your critical thinking negatively & harm your ability to concentrate. How? Well, you have all answers available just a tap away, so you no longer use your brain to solve a problem. Now your mind bears no pain, so it does have no gain! You constantly get push notifications distracting you from work and hindering your focus. Further, online activity is constantly supported with a cut in physical activity, making your body & brain inactive![57]

With full-time access to phone & social media, your mind is always pre-occupied & anxious to look for what's new. There is no "*spare & boring*" time left for thinking, which is prerequisite of a creative mind. Well, you don't worry...

... While your online environment has shaped your brain in major ways, but nothing is permanent. You can still control your online behavior.[58] Question is how should you go about this? Well, we will discuss that in subsequent sections.

14.0 Suicides & Deaths by Social Media

Firstly, I would like to make it clear that I have not over-stated anything in the above statement. There have been cases where people committed suicide or died just because of Social Media Abuse. I know it may be an unbelievable kind of statement for you. So, let me make my statement affirm with a few sad examples from the world of social media...

... Not very long ago, a 66-year-old Japanese woman became a victim of "*death by selfie*" after falling from stairs while taking selfie at Taj Mahal.[59]

While you take selfie, your mind becomes unconscious of the things around you (Have you ever noticed that?). That's the reason we find people lost in themselves while taking selfie on stairs, in lift, on escalators and everywhere else! Selfies has become a way more to "*showcase yourself*" than to "*express yourself*". All I want to say is that "*Be Careful*"! Selfie doesn't worth your life.

Selfies has become a way more to "showcase yourself" than to "express yourself".

In 2016, *The Washington Post* reported that in 2015 alone, selfie took life of at least 27 people & at least 50% of such deaths occurred in India.[60]

In another case, a teenager, who was sick of college gossip about pictures she'd sent to her male friend, whom she met in an online chat room, committed suicide by jumping in front of a train. She also left a note in which she claimed that her "*loved ones would be 'better off' without her*".[61] This is also a case of how Social Media Abuse can lead to depression, suicidal thoughts, successful suicide & ultimate death! Sadly, there are lots of other similar cases on record & perhaps countless cases which were never reported ☹.

As per *The Atlantic* report[62]:

> *"Teens who spend three hours a day or more on electronic devices are 35 percent more likely to have a risk factor for suicide, such as making a suicide plan"*

I know you are finding it hard to read all those sad things, but it's important to make you aware about the seriousness of Social Media Abuse so that you can protect yourself as well as your loved ones & people in general.

In the coming sections, we'll be discussing how to Calm Social Media & tackle these issues. As of now, we'll discuss our next issue & that is: *Financial Problems, Indebtedness & Career Crisis*. Yes, it's about money & career. I think you're excited about this one! Let's go on...

15.0 Financial Problems, Indebtedness & Career Crisis

Yes, I need to blame Social Media Abuse for financial crisis & indebtedness of some people. I was shocked when I read an article in *Business Insider* titled "*A 26-year-old woman racked up $10,000 of debt after trying to become an 'Instagram star' - and it reveals a huge issue with the platform*[63]". Yes, that's true. People are spending money to capture perfect shots for their Instagram! Some are taking loans as well!

When I hear something like this, it forces me to think how serious problem Social Media Abuse has become. I mean we need to realize that there is a world outside of online world! If you are not getting enough likes, comments or shares, that's okay! You don't need to prove anything to anybody! If you even turn out to be an internet celebrity after doing all this stuff, you'll get some money from brand sponsorships & like measures! Nothing more! As we already discussed, you need to decide if you want to make social media your business, because it's a different thing then. But for personal use, social media needs to be treated in a different manner.

On that note & with no offence to anyone, I don't think that taking loan just for an "*Instagram Click*" is a right move. We need to take care of our finances as we all have bills to pay, which are much more important than the cost of "*Instagram-perfect-pics*".

Social Media Abuse doesn't harm just personally, but professionally as well. It can bring bad reputation to your credit & effect your career & jobs badly for lifetime. There are many cases where employees have been fired[64] due to their inappropriate social media behavior like racial tweets & posts, joking about their workplace, using social media during work hours, which, obviously, are inacceptable things to any respectful organization.

If you want a little smoother career-life, you need to take care of when you use social media, what you post, what you like, what type of comments you make, what kind of language you use, what you share & whom you are following.

Further, I think that if people save time they spend on social media, they can move further in their professional & work life, get more done & earn more and get more financial freedom! *Uganda* president[65] very well pointed out:

> *"idle talk on social media is costing the country much-needed time & income"*

Though this statement was made by the *Uganda* president with reference to Uganda, it can be applied to people of all countries where social media is in use. Your social media use is costing your time & income. Your idle time spent on social media is sum total of your unpaid working hours exploited by social media companies. And guess what? Social media companies are not graceful enough to share their revenue with you even if you worked for so many hours for them on a daily basis!

Given all this, I recommend you to be a little selfish! So, cut your time on social media, save time, use it wisely & take your financial freedom & career to a next level!

16.0 Social Media: Bringing Us Together or Tearing Us Apart?

I think it's the latter! We all go to parties & gatherings and what we see is that all of us are spending more time with our phone even though the people, whom we chat with online, are around us!

We all see group of people in restaurants, picnics, even in parks: all having their eyes stick to their smartphone screens. Instead of talking to the person in front of us, we keep chatting with someone who is not with us! And guess what? Some people find this behavior "*Cool*"! Till now, I am unable to find out what's "cool" about it! I consider it "*just foolish*" ...

... Students chat in class, not real chat, but e-chat! We can do video call for hours, but we don't have enough time to meet each other in person. Clearly, social media is bringing us together but only in e-life, not in real-life!

We can have e-life & real-life both, but our emotions, health, feelings are all real. They can't be electronic! Saying hello on the phone can't replace a handshake! You can't pick your child in your hands online! Real love is real! I can very well say:

"In real life, the distance social media creates is much more than the distance it covers. Net effect is more & more distance!"

I hope that by now, you know that in disguise of bringing us together, social media is tearing us apart. Okay! I'm not imposing my opinion on you! Decide it yourself. Happy?

Now, let's explore the more of "*bad deeds*" of Social Media Abuse. Next one is *Loneliness*. Let's know more about how social media & loneliness come together...

17.0 Internet, Social Media & Loneliness

Increased use of internet has been associated with decline in social involvement & increase in loneliness[66].

Reason is simple: on social media, connections are just virtual & not real. The more time you spend online, the less time you are left with to involve yourself in real conversation with real people in real life.

You're busy with your "*internet-Phone*" & social media for all the time you're free and for all the time you're not free! In busy time, you're working with it and in free time, you're enjoying with it. As soon as you're out of your digital world, you're left with no time for a real-talk & you feel lonely.

People are busy with YouTube, Netflix, Facebook and games when they reach home – no talk with family! People are busy with their earphone while travelling, no talk with people outside. People are listening to music while taking a walk, no hello to people. Examples are countless & the fact is just one: you're busy with your gadgets all the time! The interaction in real life is going down & down.

In my own family, whenever my nieces visit home, they are busy with phones. My parents wait for them to come home & talk with them only to find that they are busy! Busy with what? Well, with watching videos and playing games. The result is less talk & a feeling of loneliness. You want to meet people & talk with them but find it hard to that as sometimes they are busy & at other times, you're busy. All that creates loneliness. You know all that. That's the case for most families now. *Loneliness is the gift of a new world which is closer than ever. Thanks to modern technology, social media, greed & our bad habits!*

18.0 Social Media, Work, Workplace & Productivity

18.1 Phones, Internet, Social Media, Gossip & Texting – Top Productivity Killers at Work

Our workplaces are so full of distractions that average office employee spends only 11 minutes between interruptions![67] Every employer wants productive employees. After all, employees are one of the major cost as well asset of any business. Apart from work, we all want to be productive in our lives to get more done, achieve more & reach as high as possible! I think it's worthy to know the biggest culprit behind your un-productivity, right? Let's know what it is...

... A study conducted by *CareerBuilder*[68] revealed Cell phone & texting as the top productivity killer at work. Gossip filled second position on the chart, while internet & social media came third & fourth respectively. It means out of top four productivity killers at work, three factors are related to smartphones & social media. *Not surprisingly*, CareerBuilder reported:

> *"One in four workers (24 percent) admitted that, during a typical workday, they will spend at least one hour a day on personal calls, emails or texts. Twenty-one percent estimate that they spend one hour or more*

> *during a typical workday searching the Internet for non-work-related information, photos, etc."*

There have been cases when employees have been caught taking selfie in the bathroom!

The study suggests that there is huge opportunity for employers to monitor the use of internet, phones & social media by their employees, if they want to increase the productivity of their employees.

Though the study conducted by CareerBuilder was in relation to workplace, I believe that it's results can be applied to other areas of life as we use social media not only at work, but in other places as well. It travels with us everywhere!

18.2 Cost of Distractions & Distracted Employees!

When we're talking about distractions, it is important to separately consider cost of distractions, which is 25 minutes per distraction![69]

Suppose, you are working on something important. Suddenly you get a call & message or check the mail in between. Do you ever think about the time cost of that call/ message? Well, it's 25 minutes each! A digital distraction study report found that it takes about 25 minutes to get back to the original task, post interruption due to any distraction. So, when you get cut off from a task (which is mostly because of social media, some not-really-urgent calls, some push notifications which are not important at all), you pay a huge time cost. It was also found that we tend to work faster to compensate the time lost due to distractions, which leave us with more frustration, stress and mental pressure. That's what makes it more important that we work with focus & Keep our phone & other gadgets away for a while when working!

Surprisingly, one 2010 research estimated that distracted workers were costing businesses $650 billion[70] per year! And I don't think that the trend is going down. Think how much money you're losing as a businessman & how much time you're losing as an employee! And when we know that most of it is caused by our phones & social media, we know the solution – "*Calm Social Media*".

Because you are already here, you're good to go! Help others & me as well by recommending "*Calm Social Media*" to your employees, employer, colleagues, friends, family & others as well! It will take few bucks from them, but it will save much more time & money as well. "*Calm Social Media*" is one of the best investment anybody can ever have, both in terms of time as well as money! (Yeah... nothing wrong in a promotion which is good for all 😊)

18.3 Social Media's Unofficial & Unpaid Employees

Sometimes, I think that all the people using social media are unofficial & unpaid employees of the social media companies. And yeah... all these employees are self-motivated, work with dedication & led by the design of Social media networks which are designed to be more & more addictive.

For some users, using social media can be a full-time job as their combined use of social media can give an average of 6 hours of use per day. This is the number of hours most people work for in a full-time job. Standard job time is 8 hours, about 1 hour is for lunch & eatables and for other 1 hour, most people just don't do office work! So, on average 6 hours a day is the number of effective hours for a full-time job. For others, who are using social media for hours, it can be considered as a part-time job.

See how generous you have become! You're working for hours for such big tech & social media giants without any pay, sacrificing your precious time, your happiness, your sleep, your health & other positive aspects of life. I think even pets would not be as much loyal to their masters as some people have become to social media. In short, they are not less than a "*social media puppet*"! Well done!

"If all people work with same dedication as they use social media with, all companies will report better performance!"

Well, if you are worried about this slavery kind of situation, don't worry! We're going to discuss the solutions shortly. Just have patience! In the meantime, let's discuss few other problems caused by Social Media Abuse...

19.0 Other Problems from Social Media Abuse & Internet

The list of issues caused by Social Media Abuse is endless. We've restricted our discussion to the most important, serious & worthy issues. In this section, we'll discuss issues other than those covered in earlier sections.

19.1 Live-Broadcast Catastrophe

Anti-social behavior on social media platforms is not an unknown issue. Use of Facebook's Live Video Streaming service for live broadcast of the shooting of a 78-year old man[71] is perhaps the biggest example of "*death of humanity*" on social media & how badly social media platforms can be harassed by "*animals in human body*"! Well, that's just one example of how disturbing & offensive it can be at times.

In another case, 4 people livestreamed a video of torture of an 18-year old man with special needs.[72] Later, hate crime, kidnapping & other charges were filed against them, but the fact that a public service, which influences more than 220 crore people now, was used for such a brutal crime, can't be changed. There are many other similar cases. If I enlist of all them here, perhaps you will leave the book aside only to read it never!

The main worry is that from children to oldies, everybody is on social media. Is it a good thing if a child see a live view of crimes like murder? I'm sure nobody wants that to happen. In fact, no one of us would like to see that in our social media feed.

19.2 Fake News & Rumors

I don't want to say much about fake news & rumors. In the world of social media, I have just two things to say here:

I. If you don't use social media for news & don't trust what's posted there, good for you. You're already on right track. Keep going like this!

II. If you depend on social media for your news & what's going on, you need to work on your "foolish habit" (yes! I said foolish habit). Don't you know that there are many authentic news apps out there? Then, why social media? Just pick some news apps & select the topics you care about, customize your feed & start reading (I have tried about 100+ news apps & all of them have customization feed options these days). One more thing, in news app, you will focus more on reading than watching those videos of cats & dogs & reading some creepy jokes! Be smart! Stop trusting social media. It will also free up "*valuable time*" of our regulators & they will be able to focus on other worthy issues of the country & the world, apart from "*how to stop fake news & rumors on social media*". This way, you'll be helping your country & the world economy as well. I hope you do the smart thing!

Further, when it comes to stop fake news & rumors, government & regulators have got a major role to play. What they can do about it? Well, will discuss it in "*Legal-Digital-Identity*" section.

19.3 Phones, Social Media, Terrible Lifestyle & "Over Smartness"

Though I am not a travel freak, but I have travelled a lot in my most beloved city 'Delhi' during my 3 years of Chartered Accountancy training. Travelling in metro was a ritual for me. During my travelling time, either I would be gazing at my Kindle App in the lust of finishing the newbie book (I proudly finished about 10 books in metro only!) or I would be staring at random people to observe their behavior. About 80% of the people seemed to be damn busy with their Smartphone. A smart look at their phones used to tell me that about 30%-50% of them are using Facebook & WhatsApp, scrolling through some useless posts while listening to music (It makes me think that Twitter is less popular in India!). How smart? Travelling, Music & Social Media all at the same time. But are they really?

While these people think of themselves as very-very smart, let me tell you that they are kinda biggest dumbs. Really. These people have hours a day to scroll through their useless social media feed, read countless jokes & view some no-brainer videos, but these people don't have couple of minutes to have an "*insightful look*" into what's going on in their social media world.

Because of such experience, I am not expecting a huge sale of this book! I know only few smart people who want to truly improve their tech and social media life, would buy and read it. But that's Okay. At least one of my dreams of expressing my thoughts on social media and impacting a few lives through it have come to life. Like you're reading this book right now! That's a big deal for me.

Yeah... I got lost there! Pardon me. Let's get back to what we were discussing. So, I was telling about people & their weird ways of using social media. Here, let me share a related incident with you...

... One evening I was coming home from office. I de-board at my station. Downstairs, I noticed one guy who had his eyes stuck on his smartphone's screen & his fingers busy with typing (Great. I too have a smartphone, but I am not smart enough to learn how to type while '*walking on stairs*'!). Well, I thought to alert him that he may fall down sometime if he continues to do that! But I didn't since I have faced very abusive language from some people due to my offering of "*Free Advice*". After all, they are smart people! To my surprise, that guy fell-off the stairs and got some serious injuries. Your tech addictions can be that harmful. Well, I felt guilty since I didn't alert him, but then I give it a second thought. I can't stand abusive language from anyone. So, perhaps, I did the right thing...

... I also find people watching movie on their phone while walking on stairs! What would you call such people? I think of them as fools! These are the people whose world is limited to their screen! I pity them ☹.

Well, these real-life stories & examples reminds us that we need to rethink our technology use. If we attach ourselves to tech like this, unwanted things can happen & that can change our lives not for good! I would like you to give a thought on how you use your phone & social media, for how much time, when, do you really need to spend so much time on it & what else you can do in place of your smartphone use.

19.4 Internet & Addiction – "Compulsive Internet Use"

Social Media, Smartphones & other gadgets work with the internet. "*Internet of Things*" is best term to describe how internet is becoming a part of more & more things connected with our lifestyle. Unfortunately, internet is very-very addictive. "*Compulsive Internet Use*"[73] ("*CIU*") is the medical name for "*internet addiction*". As we have already discussed social media part of this issue, we'll not dig it further. On a lighter note, just want to remind you again that most of the internet activities like mindless surfing the "*Google Index Bank*"[74] which has got 130+ trillion pages (out of which 100+ trillion were added in a short time span of less than 4 years from March 2013 to November 2016), scrolling through your online feeds, playing video games, time-pass chats with your so called online friends can make you feel happy temporarily & in the short-run. In the long run, you are going to make a huge loss out of it! So, be mindful.

19.5 Social Media Trolling

Have you ever seen comments & posts like "*this video sucks*", "*people who have disliked this video needs to get their brains checked-up*",

"*Somebody Noticed Donald Trump's Chin Looks Like A Frog*"?[75] Well, that's nothing but trolling!

Trolling is nothing, but "*an activity of derogatory people which involves saying or posting disrespectful, adversarial, controversial, nasty & untrue things about people, brands, companies, government or anything*".

Internet & social media are open platforms & everybody has right to speak there. The abuse of this "*right to speak*" has resulted in Internet trolling. People are using all kinds of words on Facebook, Twitter, YouTube & other social media networks with an intention to provoke people, start hate conversation or just for their evil-amusement. That's Social Media Trolling.

Today, be it a politician, celebrity, brand, government or any other person on the internet or social media, all face trolling!

If sports going on, "*bad-people*" (officially called "*trolls*") say bad things about each other's country & players. This is just one example. There are thousands of examples like this.

Personally, I don't think of trolling as a very serious issue. I think of this as simple nature: Like dogs naturally bark, some human beings also bark, perhaps due to some limitations of their own. That doesn't mean that you should bark too in return. Do the same thing you do when you come across barking dogs - stay calm & keep going!

I have come across people who use abusive language, take pleasure in upsetting others, talk disgust & have no respect for anyone. I never respond. I simply think of them as "*barking dogs with human body*". Nothing more, nothing less. It makes me feel good, ignore all the trolls & stay focused on what I am doing.

If you get upset by trolling, the purpose of trolls is complete! Do you want that? I think no. Don't pay attention to trolls. You've got much more things to worry about, right?

And yeah... if you've been in a situation of personal trolling, don't think what other people are thinking about you, as real people's thoughts don't get changed by such things. For real people: "*Trolling is simple barking*"! So, don't pay attention to it, ever.

"Trolling is simple barking"

Well, that's a personal solution. We can do a lot about it at regulatory level. Take United Kingdom for example, where trolls can face up to 2 years of imprisonment.[76] I think, other countries where such laws are not in force, need to make similar laws to deal with the situation. Will talk more about in subsequent section on "Legal-Digital-Identity", which will also deal with other Social Media Abuse & internet issues.

20.0 Smartphones: A Negative Perspective

We hear "*Be Positive*" all the time. Let's be negative about smartphone for a while to understand it's long-term negative impact on us.

20.1 Smartphone: Is It Making You Dumb?

General perception is that Smartphone makes you smart! It allows you to navigate on your own, get information with just a tap, set reminders, do shopping, play games & "*stay connected*". Well, that is brighter side of using smartphone & I'm not denying that.

On the other side, not many people know that Just having a smartphone reduces our ability to think, makes us less focused, keep us distracted & all this results in lower IQ. I don't think I need to explain the reasons behind such impacts as I believe you know it all well. Again, I will not let it go by assuming anything. So, let's be together & explore more about smartphone's problems as well as solutions...

When you have your smartphone with you (& I think you have it 24/7), you no longer feel boredom because smartphone has eliminated all the spare time you used to have. As soon as you're free from work, you turn to your smartphone to play a game, scroll through your social media feed or just mindlessly surf the web! No free time, no boredom, just work & fun! This is the case especially of the young population who have not faced the "*pre-screen era*" & spent more than 2 hours a day on social media taking the facilities available today for granted.[77] Well, boredom is not bad. It gives you time to have a look on the real world around you, have some meaningful thinking & have some peace for your mind. Being busy 24/7 is not healthy for your mind as well. Boredom is key to a creative mind. After all, your mind is most creative when you "*Just Relax, Sit Idle & Do Nothing for a While*".[78] So, if you want to maximize your creativity, learn to be bored! Boredom is one of the most important ingredient of being creative.

20.2 Are You Addicted?

Checking your smartphone is perhaps the first thing you do even before getting out of your bed in the morning! These days, no matter whom I meet, be it children/ kids, teens/ young, adults/ millennials/ Gen Y, I found each & everyone more interested in their phones than the real people! Yeah... I do feel that the elders are an exception. I still meet many elders who talk real without gazing at their smartphone when I'm with them! Smartphone is one of the biggest culprits for disrupting people in the online world. You go to café, in metro, in malls, in restaurants, at airports, in buses or cars, in a queue for whatever, you can find a live version of what I said, everywhere! Smartphone Addicts are everywhere & exception is very rare.

"Smartphone Addicts are everywhere & exception is very rare"

Well, that's a part of my opinion & thoughts on smartphone usage! Now, let's talk some data...

... As per dscout 2016 Mobile touches report, "*users tapped, swiped & clicked a whopping 2,617 times each day, on average*".[79] Going further, the number for heavy users turned out to be 5427 times. Well, I found this number insane! Have a look at this infographic...

Users tapped, swiped and clicked a whopping 2,617 times each day, on average.

HEAVY USER	AVERAGE USER
5,427 average daily touches	**2,617** average daily touches
225 average daily minutes	**145** average daily minutes

[Average Daily Touches & Time Spent on Smartphone – Study by dscout]

Can you guess which app sucked the most finger time? Well, unsurprisingly, it's Facebook. Facebook grabbed 15% share of finger time, Messaging – 11%, Instagram – 3%, Facebook Messenger – 3%, WhatsApp – 3%, Snapchat – 1%, Twitter – 1%, Hangouts – 2%, Reddit – 1%, YouTube – 1%. Means 41% of the smartphone time was spent on social media! Further, the data is for 2016. Smartphone usage is increasing all time since then. Have a look at this infographic:

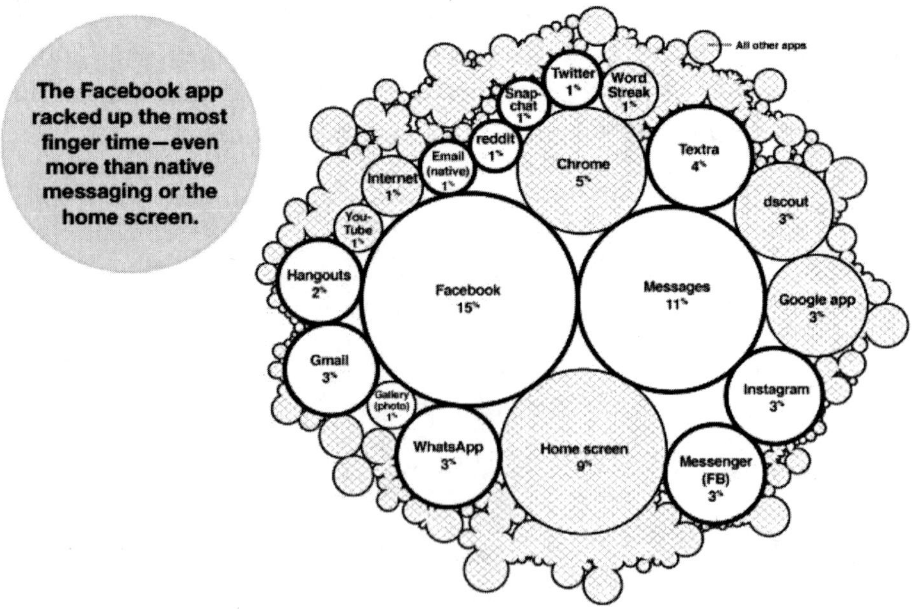

[Top 20 Apps by Share of Touches: Study by dscout]

Phone addiction has become a major issue! Lots of people are addicted to their smartphone without even knowing that they have been addicted. I have come across people who are eating with one hand and talking on phone at the same time with their second hand taking care of it! Really multi-tasking people and I don't think they are smart. These are the people who don't have time for a peaceful meal (yes meal! Forget about breakfast, lunch & dinner! It's a dream!)

As per one study, 50% of the teens feel they are addicted to smartphones. Further, 69% of parents & 78% of teens check their devices at least hourly. 72% of teens feel the urge to immediately responds to notifications & messages.[80] All these stats prove that not all. but many of us are addicted to our smartphones.

20.3 Do You own Your Phone or Does Your Phone Own You?

This question has inspired the Motorola's "*Phone-Life Balance*"[81] survey! Here are the survey results to make you aware about how deep the smartphone problem is:

- 33% of the people prefer their smartphone over spending time with their loved ones
- 53% confessed that their smartphone is their best friend (now you need to think twice before relying on the person who says that you are his/ her best friend!)
- 61% people need help with their phone-life balance (thankfully, you are not alone! Feeling relieved?).

There are several instances of people seeking treatment for nomophobia or to cure their smartphone addiction![82]

Cases have been reported where people have stolen money to buy a smartphone! And when, addicts are asked to leave their phone, their behavior can turn violent. Shockingly, some people are spending as much as 19 hours[83] on their smartphone! Can you believe this? It's mind-boggling data! In India alone, there is 75% increase in smartphone addiction cases. And yeah... that's on-record. Don't know where this number go if unreported cases are included. It shows how severe the problem is.

Well, the research suggests how much smartphone-time we spent on social media & messaging: about 50%! That represent a huge opportunity for you to cut your time on social media, save time and do better things in life.

Do you wonder how you just pick up your phone to check if there are any notifications and how your half hour is gone? Well, that's what smartphone is! Smartphone addiction is such a major issue that there is a dedicated term for it: "*nomophobia*" which is derived from the combination of these words:

"NO MObile PHOne phoBIA"

Nomophobia is a term for *"fear of being without a mobile phone.*[84] Some people are so afraid to imagine the situation of being without a smartphone that thy carry two phones to remain connected all the time.

20.4 Smartphone-Induced Brain Drain

In a research[85] conducted by *The University of Chicago*, it was revealed that:

> *"The Mere Presence of One's Own Smartphone Reduces Available Cognitive Capacity"*

It means when your smartphone is "*present with you*", it grabs your attention & reduces the attention available for doing other work. Literally, a part of your brain is drained towards your smartphone! For example, if a person is talking over phone while driving (which is unarguably wrong & nobody should use phone while driving), s/he must be driving slowly! We can't drive at the usual pace when we're talking on phone as our attention is divided between two tasks – driving & talking. If you are studying/ working & your smartphone is lying right before you, you can't have the same level of attention & focus. Don't believe it. Experiment it yourself...

... Do your work for 25 minutes with your phone away. Take a 5 minutes break (Yeah... I believe in Pomodoro). Then do your work for 25 minutes with your phone lying with you! You will notice the difference! I don't need to say more about it as I'm sure you will feel it yourself!

20.4 When People Hate You Because of Your Smartphone...

You are dining & you are busier talking on phone than talking to people who have joined you! It makes people hate you for your habits & it's just an example of inappropriate-smartphone behavior. It also shows a kinda disrespect for people you are sitting with. They may feel that their company is less worthy than the company of your smartphone. We can see this happening in social gatherings, office meetings, family get-togethers & everywhere! If you set aside your phone (which might be impossible initially) & give full attention to people when you are with them, you will notice how their behavior change towards you. Don't believe me? Well, practice this just for a day & let me know the change.

We see people driving with their eyes partially glued to their phone! Result is that in America only, distracted driving kills an estimated 9 people each day & injures 1000+ people.[86] Do you think it's smart to text while driving? I think it's ridiculous. I ask you & everyone else reading this book, to put your phone on silent mode & just don't look at this while driving as it can put not just your life in danger but the life of other people on the road & the life of your family members as well.

I have seen people bringing their phones to even washroom & talking there. Really disgusting! For people in this pity category: Just don't do it!

20.5 Smartphones Can Be Dangerous

Research found that people who spend more time with their smartphone have 27% higher chances of going into depression. More shocking finding is that people who use their smartphone for at least 3 hours a day, are much more likely to be suicidal.[87]

Today, we live with our smartphone or it can be said that our smartphone lives with us. We use smartphones from immediately upon waking up to just before going to sleep and sometimes in between as well! We wake up with our smartphone, travel with our smartphone, sleep with our smartphone, entertain with our smartphone! There is no vacation for smartphone! Perhaps, our smartphone becomes busier when we go on vacation. After all, on vacation more photos are clicked, more posts are shared & more videos are recorded.

20.6 Smartphones Can Make You Sad

Using smartphone for too long, obsessive use of social media can cause depression & add to your stress making you sad! With reference to smartphone, *Cary Cooper*, Professor of *Organizational Psychology and Health* at *Lancaster University* said[88]:

> *"Like television, the light draws you in and numbs your senses. It's the exercise equivalent of treading water and can be both addictive and destructive in the way it occupies your mind without actually stimulating it"*

20.7 Deal With It

You already knew that how many good things smartphone brings to your life! Now, you also know that how much negativity it adds to your life! I'm sure, you must be willing to tackle this. Great! We'll discuss smartphone-solutions in the subsequent sections of Calm Social Media. Just wait for it!

As of now, let's explore my experiments on social media:

21.0 My Experiments with Social Media

21.1 No WhatsApp for 33 Days!

When I was using WhatsApp, I used to receive frequent notifications & due to frequent use of my phone in content writing, I used to read all notifications in about real time.

Since, read receipts are sent (I know there is option to disable read receipts, but I need read receipts from others! So, can't do that.), there is pressure to reply instantly. Result is shifted focus from my current work to draft the reply & hit that send button. That causes more *task-switching*: a major halt to productivity! As per study, *it takes about 25 minutes to get back to the original task post interruption due to any distraction.*[89] And to add more trouble, such distractions causes us to work faster to compensate the time lost, leaving us with more frustration, stress and mental pressure...

... On 2nd May 2018, I decided to take a break from WhatsApp for at least a month! I sent message to all my contacts informing them that I will be no longer available on WhatsApp & have switched to Signal App (citing security as the issue to keep the experiment private!) ...

... Then I deleted WhatsApp from my phone! Well, among all experiments, it was the toughest one as all my contacts were using WhatsApp (which is a usual thing for all of us). Now I was disconnected from all of them. What happened next? Let's explore...

... Well, it was a "*dual-taste experience*"! I started using traditional "SMS" service again for short messages & mail for other things. In the WhatsApp world, fewer people use SMS service & the result was a total cut in time-wasting messages. Now, I was not getting any funny messages, jokes, quotes or videos on my phone. There were fewer notifications in my phone. All text messages I got were work related only. And yeah... as far as "*connectivity*" is concerned, I was still connected with people I care about on call or in person. But, now I was not distracted every few minutes. So, I got quite good results! Well done! Now, let's see the down side of this approach...

... Being unavailable on WhatsApp resulted in some funny incidences & communication issues as well. When I met new people during this experiment phase, as usual. they asked for my WhatsApp number & when I told them that *I'm not on WhatsApp*, they looked me like I'm a person from another planet! Some people greeted me with their cunning smile as well (perhaps thinking of me as a dumb person & tech disabled man!). Anyway, I decided to continue my experiment despite these issues...

... A few contacts were using only WhatsApp & took email as a nightmare. I was not able to contact them properly when it comes to sharing media & documents. Also, I got complaints that sending a mail each time is more time consuming & uncomfortable, asking me to switch back to WhatsApp. While there are lots of other messaging apps available that support all kinds of messages, but majority of people were not using them. Clearly, I felt the need to download

WhatsApp again to keep communication in flow. So, I again downloaded WhatsApp on 5th June 2018...

... 33-days of WhatsApp experiment was over & I was on WhatsApp again, but my mindset was changed in one major way. Let's discover that...

... Earlier, I used to check WhatsApp each time some notification land in my phone. The mind was programmed in that way. One-month halt in that process gave my mind a break & now there was no force to check the messages in real time. I disabled WhatsApp notifications & now check WhatsApp just 2-3 times a day. The result is less distraction, more productivity, more time to do things I want to do in life. And yeah... don't worry about important messages as if it's that important, people can simply call you & ask you for your response!

So, feel free to repeat this experiment yourself. You'll learn a lot. That's my promise. If you don't want to take risk of deleting WhatsApp for so long, try a short duration experiment. Want fewer risk? Okay. Try disabling WhatsApp notifications & check for messages on a fixed time only. It's worth your effort! Happy Experimenting!

21.2 Facebook – The Apex Time-Evil App, Disabled!

Yeah... Facebook! You know about it all, right? Facebook is the social media leader eating most of your screen time.

No wonder, my "*yet another*" experiment was to disable Facebook app. I was convinced that Facebook is the "*apex time-evil app*". So, I decided to delete it from my phone. And then I learnt a new thing! Facebook comes pre-installed in your phone & it can't be deleted (seriously!). No problem. There is "*disable*" option as well in phone's app settings. I quickly disabled the Facebook app & it's one of the best decisions I have ever took.

I did it in September 2017 & the experiment is ongoing till now! Yeah... I re-enabled Facebook a couple of times for very short durations but that was not for personal purpose, it was simply to explore more about Facebook to help me writing this book. It has helped me a lot in cutting time I used to spent on Facebook. Now, I do check my profile & page occasionally in browser & it take not more than 5 minutes a week. I no longer have to see that blue icon calling me to check it! Life is much better now!

21.3 Facebook Messenger – Out for Ever!

I say: "*The less social media, the better*"! Yes, I believe it. It goes same for the social media apps as well. The less social media apps, the better. It simplifies social life, save phone's storage, internet & time!

This is the perfect time to discuss why I deleted Facebook Messenger from my phone & why you should too. Well, I just thought that all my contacts who are using Facebook Messenger are using WhatsApp as well, but all the contacts who are using WhatsApp, are not using Facebook Messenger. Then, what's the point of using Facebook Messenger? (Yeah... there may be some exclusive features in Facebook Messenger, but all the messaging features I need, are there in WhatsApp) So, I decided to delete Facebook Messenger.

It was the easiest of all things I have done to Calm Social Media. At least, I'm no longer part of useless group conversations there in the messenger! Good for me. If you have not done it, do it! It's the easiest task on your Calm Social Media To-Do-List!

22.0 How to Calm Social Media?

Tips, tricks, measures, methods, hacks or say it whatever you want, to help you quit or cut social media from your life!

Now you know how Social Media is affecting your life in negative ways. You also know that the cause of Social Media Abuse is within you or the people with whom you are "*connected*". To change ourselves as well as whom should we connect with, is in our hands, right? Yep!

Then what are we waiting for? Well, we are waiting for a note! It's here (just finish this & then we will proceed to explore how to Calm Social Media):

Note: Tips, tricks, measures, methods, hacks or *say it whatever you want*, mentioned in this section are applicable to all social media networks in general. It will also help you in cutting your time on internet & gadgets. After going through this section, we'll discuss some social media "*network-specific*" tips in subsequent sections. Okay?

Let's act now to control our social media & related habits and make our digital & real life better with Calm Social Media:

22.1 Make Sure You Want to Do It!

When we use/ hear the words like willpower, it sounds so philosophical & to me it sounds so much practical as well. Why?...

... Because lack of willpower is cited as the No.1 reason for not making the changes required for living a healthy lifestyle[90]!

> *"The power of your will is one of the strongest power you can have in your quiver"*

If you are willing to do what is right, you will have most important barrier to change i.e. *lack of willpower*, removed from your difficult path. So, first you need to make your mind ready for it! For this, it's important that you understand why you need to cut your time on social media (Since you have managed to read Calm Social Media Book so far, I believe you understand it very well!). Then think about the benefits you'll get if you opt for the right change (like in case of social media, if you restrict your social media use, you'll have more time to do quality things in life, you can do more work or just involve in some recreational & much useful activities, which are much better than social media activities).

Once you have your mind prepared to Calm Social Media, you will be able to follow subsequent Calm Social Media steps and come out of *Social Media Trap* very easily.

22.2 Just Make Yourself Unable to Log into Your Social Profiles

Well, you need guts for doing that. Just ask one of your friends or family members to change password and email ID connected with your social accounts without telling you! Once you do that, you'll not be able to log into your old social profiles anymore! It will make you disconnected from at least your old social profiles.

You can argue that you can build new profiles. Yes, you can but those new profiles don't feel the same and doesn't get the same attention as the previous ones. Old is Old!

My experience with this trick: Well, I was unable to use this method as I had several business pages connected with my Facebook profile (& other social media networks were not a problem for me), but I am fortunate enough for being a self-controlled person & was able to take control of my social media very well. I didn't need this method. But yeah... I have tried other methods to cut my time on social media to about just 7 minutes a week. Yes, it's one minute a day. I don't think that social media (excluding meaningful conversation) deserves more time than that.

22.3 Make Yourself Undiscoverable!

Don't worry! I'm not telling you to leave the "*typical world*" & go on to mountains!

Many Social media profiles have the option to let others find you by your email & phone number associated with your account. It results in increasing friend requests & following from "*unreal, fake friends & followers*". You'll simply be wasting your time by looking at those notification numbers. What's the hack?

Just make it difficult for others to find you with your email & phone number! Most of the social media sites have such option. And on how to do it, my answer is: *Just Google it*! Otherwise, I need to fill this book with really great tech stuff!

My experience with this trick: I have tried this tip for my Facebook & Twitter profiles & I found a drop-in friend requests I used to have. So, it works well.

And yeah... you don't need to worry about losing a precious friend as if a friend is precious to you & care about you, he will discover other means to connect with you. Remember, when there is a will, there is a way!

22.4 Turn-off Push Notifications

One of the most useful method I have ever experienced! I have Business accounts on Twitter, Facebook and Instagram, so I was not able to uninstall the apps from my phone. I founded another trick - block notifications from disturbing apps!

Just switch to app settings page in your device settings & block the notifications. You will get much-much relief. Don't know the steps for how to do it? Well again, *just Google it*!

22.5 Uninstall Social Media Apps

This is the best way to solve the entire problem! It's simple, easy to implement & take just seconds! Well, believe it or not, this solution is easier said than done. It takes courage & determination to hit the uninstall or disable button for the apps you are spending a huge time on...

... Even harder test starts after you delete the apps. Why? Because you have 24/7 internet access. Your phone is in your hands & re-installation is just a tap away. Here comes the test of how disciplined & determined you're.

To stop yourself from re-installing the app, you must have a control on yourself, else this method will not work. You'll keep just deleting & re-installing apps. So, how can you keep your attention away from social media? Well, for this, you need to keep yourself busy in some good activities. You'll find many options for such activities as we go ahead with Calm Social Media discussion.

22.6 Use Grayscale Mode: Turn Your Phone Black & White

Firstly, let me tell you that this trick is not mine but Tristan Harris, Former Design Ethicist at Google.[91]

It's obvious that colors like black & grey are not as attractive to our eyes as colors like yellow, blue, red, especially when used with contrasting colors like white.[92] That's why most of the apps & websites use these colors for their app & website icons to attract your attention...

... When you look at your phone's screen & see icons of apps like Snapchat (combination of yellow, white & black), YouTube (combination of red & white), Facebook (combination of blue & white), WhatsApp (combination of green & white), Instagram, Twitter, et cetera, these instantly attract you!

What if your entire phone turns black & white? Well, in that case, you will find your phone "*less glamourous*". It will not be as attractive as it was before. Grayscale option is readily available in your smartphone. Just go to "*Vision settings*" under "*Accessibility settings*" & tap the grayscale option. Your entire phone will turn into black & white. If you need technical help for how to use this option, just Google: "*Change Your Screen to Grayscale*".

Once your phone is in grayscale mode, you'll feel the same way as if your color TV has been replaced with Black & White TV ("*B&W*" for "*cool*" people!). Now, your phone is less attractive to you & you will use it less! At least give it a try! If you don't like it, no worries! you can switch back with just a tap!

22.7 Challenge Yourself Publicly & Take a Public Social Media Detox!

If we don't go fancy about meaning of *Digital Detox*, it simply means a break from being online.

Internet enabled gadgets are so much accessible that everybody seems connected 24/7. We are permanently online.

No secret, being online all the time & taking care of so many profiles & accounts sucks a lot of your time and energy (physical as well as mental). Wouldn't it be a better idea to unplug yourself from your devices & take a leap from internet? *Say Goodbye* to Social Media. Okay, try it at least for a few days. You know, people have already tried it, and few loved it so much that they decided to permanently quit social media. They felt more relaxed, calm, fulfilled & productive.

Now, you must be thinking that going on a "*Social Media Leave*" is a very tough task. How should you go about this? Don't worry. I have got a solution...

... Make a public post that you are leaving social media for some specific period of time (say for a month!). Now all your friends & followers know that you have accepted a challenge! If you want your reputation to continue, you need to win your challenge. If you lose, you know what's going to happen, right? You'll be called a loser & you'll have to face lots & lots of embarrassment! You'll not let that happen. I'm sure. So, go for a digital detox publicly! Give it a try at least. It's one of the best methods I can suggest.

22.8 Don't Pass Time! Find A Higher Purpose.

Browsing internet randomly or using social media while standing in a queue or waiting in public places, while travelling & in the entire so-called free time is common now. While a few minutes of such activity can be understood as refreshing but spending much time & all time-gaps on these activities is totally no-brainer. Some people call it time-pass! Non-sense!

By time-pass, I remember one interesting incident. Let me tell you about it...

... This incident too happened in Metro. I was going home after a *not-so-long* workday & as usual, I was travelling without earphones (as I am among those few stupid travelers who don't carry earphones while travelling). So, my ears had to bear what other are talking (or music other are playing!) ....

... Anyway, let's continue with the incident I was telling you about...

... So, I was going back to home. As it was evening time, metro was overcrowded! Soon after boarding the train, I overheard something. One girl was there travelling with a guy standing right after me and she was talking really nonsense and that too very loud (may be that guy had got some hearing issues!). Among other things, the girl said to him:

> *"Time-pass करने के लिए कुछ-न-कुछ तो ढूंढ़ना पड़ता है।"*
> [English:*To pass the time, there is something to find.*]

... After overhearing that statement, I looked at her smartphone and got to know that she was extremely busy with her Facebook feed!

I quoted this incident here, not to make fun of someone or to humiliate somebody, but because there is something very important, we can learn from what that traveler said. And that thing is, "*type of life*" in terms of purpose: "*Purposeless Life*" & "*Purposeful Life*" ...

... Those who don't have any purpose in life, pass their time. They do what others (including social media) want them to. They are the followers...

... While those who have some purpose in life, utilize their time. They do what they want to. They are the leaders. In which category you want to be, that's up to you.

Decide on to something you want to achieve in life & "*never settle*". When you live a purposeless life, anybody and anything can waste your time. Social media is best in doing that. Whenever, "*people without purpose*" are free or traveling (even with someone), they tend to scroll their social media feed as such people don't have a purpose. They have nothing meaningful to do with their time and think that it's fun to have a look at what's going on in their social feed.

I think there are lots of other activities you can do & which are far better than gazing at your phone. I know you want me to quote some activities here, right? Sure, Yes! Here we go:

Just carry a book with you & start reading whenever you get some free time or just sit back, relax & do nothing, just observe the environment & people around you! You would wonder to know that our mind is most creative when we are doing nothing...

... It's a concept called 'Default Mode Network' (DMN).[93] According to this concept, when your brain is not focused on some particular task, it is in *autopilot mode* and certain brain parts become more active in that mode leading to creative thinking. So, whenever you get a chunk of free minutes, just don't think, sit idle and let your brain rest. Actually, your brain does never rest even in rest mode, rather it may be more active when it's unfocused & can come up with something creative for you that can make you brilliant! Smart approach, right?

22.9 There Are Even Better Apps & Websites than Social Media

If you are just eager to spent time with your smartphone or laptop, that's fine. Just spend it smartly. Digital world has got you covered for it. There are much better apps you can spend your time on & learn something meaningful...

... There are news apps, apps to learn code, apps to sharp your tech skills, apps to learn web designing, graphic designing, learn cooking & the list of endless options continues... Probably there is app for everything & anything you are passionate about. Isn't it a good idea to advance your skills with in-app or online learning & take your career to a next level.

Further, the more you learn, the more thinking capabilities you have. It opens up your mind & the door for more opportunities for invention & innovation! Sounds great, right? So, download apps about things you care about & you can make a career out of it or just compliment your existing career with more skills, knowledge & an open mind.

22.10 Think About the Lost Fun

Take a break to think about what would you do if you have no social media......?

Did you take the break & give it a thought? Yep! Well done!

While we can't have a chat right now, but you can drop a mail to me telling your thoughts. I would love to know that. At the moment, let's take a look at my take on this...

... I think your excessive social media use is making you miss some very precious things, moments & fun you could have (or better, you can have) in your life like hanging out with friends (offline i.e. in person and not online), pursuing a hobby, spending time with family, go out for exercise & take part in sports, better relations with people in real life, excel in study & work.

If you cut your time on social media, you'll be able to get back these precious things in your life.

Think about it. It will make you come back on the right path!

22.11 There Are Alternative Ways to Stay Connected!

Social Media is neither beginning, nor end of the world! Also, it's not the only way to keep in touch with your loved ones! There are many more ways to stay connected. A few can be simple calling, meeting them in person, arranging get-togethers or other ways to increase "*real-connectivity*".

Personally, I use to call or meeting in person. If you have better ideas, do let me know. Will list the best ones on CalmSocialMedia.com.

22.12 Do Some Outdoor Activities

No online activity can replace outdoor activities. Involve yourself in swimming, running, cycling, gardening, or just take a simple walk. Outdoor activities are much rewarding than online activities. Try it once & you'll love it over your social media activities.

22.13 Saying NO to Your Social Media Craving

I know that it's not easy to say no to something in which you have put so many precious hours of your life in so many years! Think about long term goals; write them on paper & keep that paper with you. Each time you have social media craving, open that paper & read that. It's a proven self-help way. I have used this....

... I designed my laptop & mobile screen myself. I wrote my proposed company name on it along with its logo! Each time I feel the craving to do some time-wasting activity, I just look at that wallpaper of my desktop or mobile (whatever I have at that moment) & those little things reminds me that I have much higher things in life to work for. Currently I have "*I'm Skyward Bound*" (that's my next project) wallpaper (designed by me, of course) set on my screen. This is just one way I stop myself from involving in time-wasting activities!

"I'm Skyward Bound"

I believe in science, I believe in experiments, I believe in research & so I believe in power of written goals. Written goals have a visual impact on our brain that makes our brain work actively to achieve our goals & we have 42% more chances to achieve goals that are written! That's how our brain works! So, do write your goals.[94]

Second thing I use is lists! Yep! I said lists. Lists can do amazing things in life. I make list of all my passion as well as professional projects. A look at those lists reminds me of how many things are yet to be done & how short I'm on time! Every second is precious. I can't waste any of it. And yeah... all this process makes me more & more confident, proud & I get a feeling of satisfaction of controlling my life on my own! We all are free & we should use our liberty wisely. We need to make right choices, choose right paths, take actions & avoid multi-tasking. Oops! I said, "*avoid multi-tasking*"! Pardon me! I said the wrong thing as *multi-tasking* doesn't exist...

[Multitasking - Illustration by Serena Wong[95] at Pixabay]

.... In disguise of multi-tasking we are just doing task-switching – picking another task before completing the first or simultaneously doing two tasks, like talking on phone & checking emails at the same time. With task-switching, you are able to fool your brain that you are fulfilling much more work in single time and your brain rewards you more by increasing the release of dopamine, which makes you feel happy.[96]

Study has found that so called "*multi-tasking*" leads to 40% loss in your productivity because it can take up-to 25 minutes to focus on the original task after switching from the another one. So, if you want to be productive & get more done, Be Smarter! Stick to single-tasking.[97] Finish one task before switching to next one. Say *Big No* to multi-tasking. In short, I remember all this in one line: "***own choices, own paths, one action at one time***"!

22.14 Don't Feel Guilty

"You can't erase the past, but you can act at present & make your future"

Realization about how much time you have wasted on social media & bad internet habits can leave you with a feeling of guilt. You might start thinking "*what-what else*" you could have done in that time. Well, that thought of you is right, but useless at the same time. You can't erase the past, but you can act at present & make your future. Just think about how you can change your habits now to build a better future. This approach is smart & pragmatic as well (I hate the word "practical" as it's abused by lots of people out there!).

22.15 Do Exercise

We feel good when we use social media. While feeling good is good, social media does not do anything good to our minds. And once you are there, only you know how much time it will take to stop scrolling!

Well, if you want to just feel good, why don't involve in activities that don't just make you feel good but also add value to life? Exercise is the first on my list. Next time whenever you are eager to use social media, turn off your phone & go for a walk instead. It would make you feel much better.

-Fun Fact-

Do you know that Just 15 minutes of exercise per day can increase your life by 3 years? Bonus part is that it will also reduce the chances of cancer by 1% and chances of death by 14%. Want more life? Exercise for 30 minutes a day which can add about 4 extra years to your life. in case of exercise, we can say that less is not more & more is better! GO ON! Engage yourself in walking, running, cycling or any other exercise and live more![98]

22.16 Don't Pretend

Pretend: That's what a lot of people do with their phones. Even if you are not busy, you pretend to be so to let others get a false impression about you that you are a very busy person...

... Well, just try to impress yourself because:

The day you will be able to impress yourself, you'll be able to impress the whole world!

22.17 A Goodbye to Instant Gratification

In the online world, every service is just a tap away & you can avail the services you want any-time-all-time! There is no waiting time & habitually you just can't wait! We think just short-term & want immediate benefits & enjoyment, ignoring long-term goals. That's what Instant gratification is!

In the pre-phone world, people used to write letters to each other & a reply could take days given the postal time! And now... we have instant messenger services available 24/7. You can connect with anyone anytime, can shop with a click. What's the result? Zero patience! Today, we want everything instantly. We can't wait for long! Take Pizza for example. 30 minutes. You will go mad if it crosses that 30 minutes mark, right? If Facebook is down for a second, news about it will be read for hours.

With social media, the problem of instant pleasure has become more complex. To grab instant rewards, you give up on what you are doing! Like, you can't stop yourself from checking the notification that just landed in your phone! As soon your phone rings, you forget your current work & check for the notification! Social Media is exploiting it & it's the major threat to what you want to achieve in life. Your brain has been programmed in ways that you can't stop yourself from getting instant relief.

We give up on the tough work for short-term pleasures & unearned leisure time. Checking Facebook or watching that new movie seems to be more relaxing than preparing for the exams next month or completing that pending project! Social Media companies are smart enough to exploit your "Instant Gratification" weakness & send you as much push notifications as they can.

Well, that's how you are used in the online world! You waste your time on no-brainer services of others. If you don't want to be exploited further, learn to delay your gratification. Keep yourself busy with mindful activities. Delayed gratification will not only help you Calm Social Media, but also help in other areas of life. Like by saying no to mindless shopping, you can save for future & better retirement. You can pick-up your phone at set intervals & check all notifications at once instead of checking each one of them separately. It will lead to less distractions & more productive life.

22.18 Leave Social Media Aside & Use Best Ways to Follow Brands, Topics, People & Catch News

I have already said it, but there is no harm to have it in the list of dedicated tips & tricks to Calm Social Media. If you, like many others, use social media to stay on the top of news & what's going on, you are NOT on the right track! Firstly, there is fake news & rumors issues with social media & secondly social media is not smart's place to catch what's going on...

... There are dedicated news & other apps where you can follow topics, brands & people you care about. Since dedicated apps are authentic, you will also get cured from fake news! I am not going to tell you which ones you should use. You can explore the best ones for you! If you want me to suggest which ones you should use or want to know which ones I use, just let me know about it, I will do a long post on the topic along with my review.

22.19 Check It in Browser at A Fix Time

They always say that it's better with the app & that they are constantly updating their app to make your experience "*even better*" (or "*addictive*", as per my understanding). Well, I agree with "*them*".

So, what's the hack here? You take your social media experience to a level, "*lower than better*". I mean, just delete the social media apps & use social media in your browser...

... Believe it or not, having those social media app icons on the front of your screen is like having a psychological enemy with you! Don't do it! Don't feed your enemy...

... Deleting the apps & using browser only will help you to keep the social media temptation away. And yeah... don't keep checking social media. Just decide a fix time for it. Okay?

22.20 Content We Consume Shape Our Thoughts: Mind It!

Your thoughts are made up of what you see, what you watch, what you hear. Content you consume on social media (or on the internet & elsewhere) has a great role in framing your mindset, how you think & what you do. It impacts your entire personality. So, be mindful of what type of people you connect with on social media & what you read & watch there!

22.21 Social Media, Vacation & Your Safety

If you are even little bit aware about social media world, you'll agree that almost everybody who is on vacation seems to post photos & videos of airports, planes they are boarding, their hotel room, the food they are enjoying, the shopping malls they are checking into & blah, blah, blah – all in real time! Okay! I'm glad they're happy, but I am also worried for a concern probably these people are not aware about! I'm talking about relationship between vacation pics on social media & your safety. You might be thinking what kind of bizarre relationship this is. Well, let me explain...

... Social media is an open space & when you post your vacation or travel pics in real time, your friends & other people who knows you (including some bad guys out there) know that you are far away from home. In your absence, such bad guys may target your home for their next robbery or other like activities.[99] So, why take risk? Just snap the pictures. Keep those in your phone & post them when you are back! Smart & safe approach, right? So, Post smart! Be safe!

22.22 Ask Yourself: Do I Read What I share?

On average, we read just 20% text of a web page.[100] Wondering why? It's simple –we don't have time to read every word written on that page & we just efficiently scan the web-page to find the information we are looking for.[101]

Did you notice that time is a factor for why we don't read the entire information of a page? Then how we get time to share the information for which we don't have time to read? Think about it.

It's "*sharing more, reading less*" kind of situation! There have been cases where people share something just by looking at its headline! We learn by reading, not sharing. Some people try to outsmart others by sharing smart content on their social media profiles even without reading it. These people don't even know that they are just wasting their time. It's just a matter of minutes when the content you just shared would be buried under countless posts shared by other users. You don't get anything out of it, but if you had invested your sharing time in reading or learning something useful, it would have added something meaningful to your personality.

From morning selfie to breakfast pics to Good Night post, people share "*lots of things*" and much of it is just a piece of nonsense! Sometimes, content is shared just to prove that you are reading stuff on the web & you are not missing out, right? But wait for a second! Think how much of that stuff you actually read.

Well, as per one study, it's just 41%. Yep! About 51% links on social media are shared by users without even checking the content (for them just heading is sufficient to make the content share worthy).[102] That's where time goes. Instead of devoting your time to reading, you are "*wasting*" it in sharing stuff that perhaps nobody is reading (after all, not many of us have huge following). Well, this leads to reduced information & is a signal of how dumb one can be! People feel that sharing is free. Well, it's not as huge time cost is involved in it. Share 10 things and your 10-15 minutes are gone. Then you will look for how many likes, comments or retweets it has got: another time-wasting factor. Smart people read more & share less on "*social media*". Decide your category yourself!

22.23 Gaming, Children & Parenting: Wake-up Call

Gone are the days when only adults used to have smartphones. In the world of internet, more & more younger children either have their own smartphones/ laptops or access their parents'! For what? Well, mostly to play games or watch videos & *stay connected*! While there is no harm in children playing games or having fun with videos! After all, childhood should be fun. But there are concerns that can't be ignored. Games (especially video games), YouTube, Netflix, Candy Crush & other like services are highly addictive for children (& everyone else!).[103]

Few minutes screen time is good but if children have their eyes fixed on the screen for hours, there is a problem we need to tackle. There are cases when children have been sent to rehab after addiction development. I'm not kidding. You may find it hard to believe, but it's true! Recently, a 9-year-old girl was sent to rehab due to her *gaming addiction*. Reportedly, she was playing a game called "*Fortnite*" for 10 hours a day & when her father tried to take it away from her, she hit her father![104] That's the finest example of how serious this issue can become!

If you have kids with same issues, please take care of the issue. Ask them to cut their digital activity time & engage in physical gaming & other fun activities. If your kids have not yet developed such problems, give yourself a pat on the back for your parenting skills & make sure that your kids develop good habits in future too!

22.24 Don't Cut Your Sleep for Screen Time

I often say this borrowed line (don't know from whom I did borrow it! I just remember it!):

If sleep were a credit card company, most of us would be indebted!

Social Media & smartphones has a lot of contribution to your sleep deprivation. In a study reported by *Daily Mail Online*, expert said that Social Media & smartphones are so stressful that now you need more than 8 hours of sleep. [105] It was found that in the modern world, we process huge volume of information which makes us more stressed out & now we need 8.5 hours of sleep. Screen light of our smartphones, laptops & tablets has a contribution to sleeplessness. The result is widespread sleep-debt.

Sleep debt is the difference between hours of sleep you should be getting & the hours you actually sleep for! And yeah... add the difference for the last 365 days! The total you get is your sleep debt. Got the point? Normally, 7-9 hours of sleep is considered healthy, but when you cut on your sleep time on a daily basis (given your busy lifestyle, I understand!), it leads to sleep deficit. Sleep debt is a widespread problem now. Take America for example, where 1 in 3 people are suffering from sleep deficit![106] This is huge number.

Sleep deprivation is the major reason why you feel tired all the time. After healthy diet & regular exercise, sleep is considered as third pillar of a healthy life. Your body needs proper sleep. You know where you spend your time (perhaps on web surfing, social media & like activities! I'm not saying that, but research[107]). Cut your time on such useless activities & don't compromise on your sleep time. Sleep well. Live well!

22.25 Don't Be A Product of Social Media Companies!

When a product is free, you are the product. The statement is very valid for social media service. You use all these services for free & your time or your attention is sold by social media companies in exchange for advertising revenue. Well, you know that & I don't see any harm in that. But greed is not good, right? Now, unfortunately, greed is what most social media companies are led by...

... In the lust of making you spend more time on their platforms, most social media companies are trying to make their services as addictive as they can. Frequent push notifications, sending *activity* emails, forcing browser users to install apps: all these factors show that today, social media companies care about many things, but the most they care about is money, and that too at your "*emotional expense*".

It would not be wrong to say that today majority of social media companies wants people to be a puppet of their service. But yes, it is important to add here that not all are same.

While few companies like Google & Apple are taking effort to make users aware about their excessive use of social media & smartphones (like YouTube has come up with a "*take-break reminder*" feature & Apple is rolling out an update to let users know how much time they spent on each app), but companies like Facebook, Instagram and Snapchat seem to worry about how to keep you hooked for more & more time. Whenever I check Facebook in my mobile browser, I get "*Try Facebook for Android*" notification all time, no matter how many times I tap on that cross button! Have a look at how Facebook is forcing me and everybody who has disabled the app:

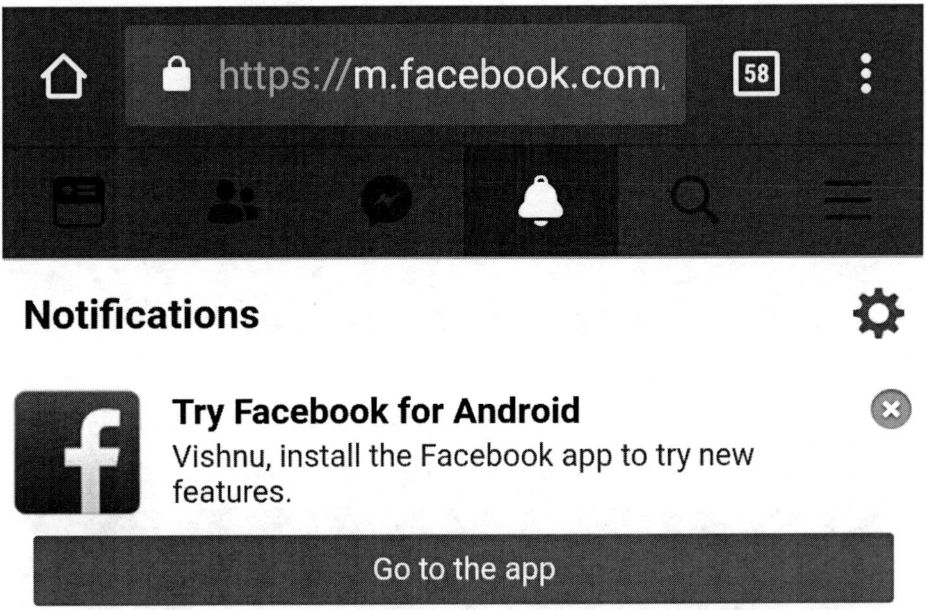

[Facebook Forcing Users to Install Facebook App with Repeated Notifications - Calm Social Media]

Every time, I check Facebook, "*Never lose a message*" notification prompts me to install messenger, no matter how many times I tap on that close button! I think Facebook doesn't understand that "*No means No*". Have a look at Facebook's repeated notification here:

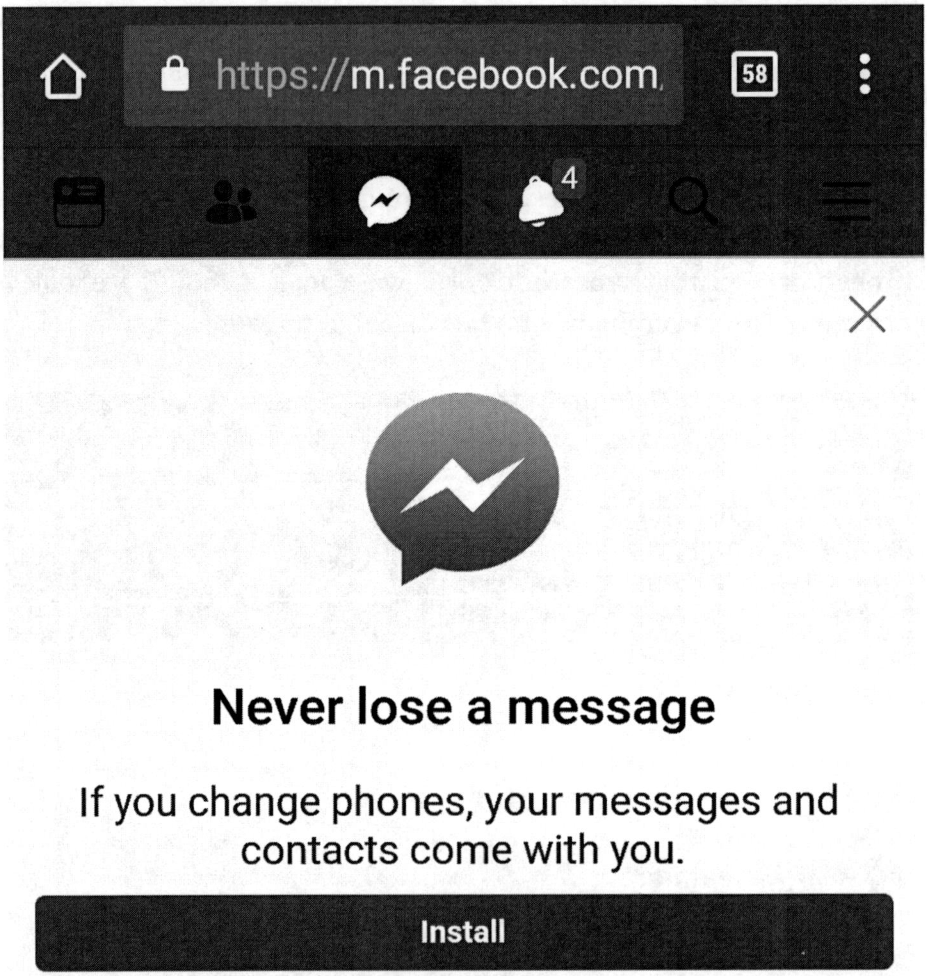

[Facebook Forcing Users to Install Messenger with Repeated Notifications - Calm Social Media]

Among Facebook, Instagram, Snapchat, Twitter & YouTube, the first 3 are the worst apps in terms of how much time you spent & how much negativity (excess of negativity over positivity) you get!

I think we have given these companies the liberty allowing them to fool ourselves. Especially Facebook & Instagram, which are famous for their apologetic leadership, will continue to sell your time to advertisers (in disguise "*Bring the World Closer Together*"), if you don't control your use of these networks.

22.26 No Addiction Is Addiction in Fact. You Were Born Free! Be Free!

It's a philosophical take on addiction & obsession and it needs to be included here as it works. At times, we can feel that we have become a slave of our bad habits, that includes Social Media Abuse as well! At the same time, we can find people who were in worse situation than us at some point of time in their life & how they hit harder! If you think quitting Facebook, Instagram, Candy Crush or being without your smartphone is a big deal, don't worry!

It may be a big deal for you but not the impossible one! There are people who have been able to take control of their Social Media Abuse & now living a real-social-life! You need to understand one thing: "*No Addiction & habit is bigger & powerful than you*". We are human beings – the most powerful creature of the nature. We can control every aspect of our life! So yeah... we all were born free. So, why compromise our freedom because of social media or anything else! Just be free!

22.27 Don't Use Smartphone & Don't Read E-Books at Sleep Time

Most people (perhaps you too!) like to read books at night to help them fall asleep. But if you are using e-Books at night instead of print books, beware! Light emitting from e-Books you are reading before your bedtime makes it tougher for you to fall asleep and reduces the next morning alertness letting you feel sleepier in daytime and adversely impact your health & performance. Smart approach is to use only print books at night to enjoy deep sleep.[108]

Similar case goes with smartphone. Reason is, smartphone screen light has similar effect like sunlight which makes it hard to get to sleep as well as stay asleep.[109] Even teens & children are losing sleep time & sleep quality due to excessive use of smartphones and tablets. It is recommended not to use smartphone & other electronic devices at least one hour before going to sleep for better sleep at night and an "*alert & productive day ahead*"!

22.28 Use A Bedtime Alarm!

For proper sleep, it's important that we unplug our devices at least an hour before going to bed. While most of us set up a morning alarm, perhaps no one of us set up a bedtime alarm![110] Do you? Well, you should. Set up an alarm to buzz at least an hour before your bedtime. And yeah... set it for the same time each night as it will alarm you to unplug all your gadgets before going to bed, so that you can have a better sleep.

Screen time just before going to sleep can harm a good sleep & bedtime alarm can help with that. Also, you should go to bed at the same time each night. After all, having a routine is the utmost need of a productive life. So, have a "*Morning Alarm*" and have a "*Bedtime Alarm*"!

22.29 Now-Me versus Future-Me

We delay our actions all the time! You say: Okay, from tomorrow I will not use Facebook so much, I will not check my WhatsApp and Twitter so frequently. And that tomorrow become your next today. The "*future-me*" in you become never true. Think about it. Solution is simple: you need to avoid procrastination. I am not going to guide you on procrastination. I will just say: *Act now*.

22.30 Ask One Harsh Question: Do You Want to Remain A Social Media Puppet for Life?

Ask Yourself:

"Am I puppet of social media?"

Well, When I was struggling with my addiction to social media, I used to think like that – *I am not a puppet of social media.* If I am addicted to social media, I am in kinda social media prison. We were born to live free, then why limit yourself? Remember, if you are not in control of yourself, you are not free. If Social media controls your habit, you are not free even in a free world. Same applies to your rest of the addictions as well (I wish you don't have any!).

So, if you're not a social media puppet, good for you. But, if you're, Just *Calm Social Media*! Then, social media will be puppet of you!

22.31 Understand Your Self-Worth

Some people call themselves down to earth, humble. They listen to others! If you're among them, fine. It's good that you are such a positive person. That's one side of this approach. There are people as well who consider themselves "*smart*" (though they are not!), who make use of so-called "*down to earth*" people, considering them as fool.

Being "*down to earth*" & being "*fool*" are two different things. You don't need to be a "*fool*" to be a "*down to earth person*". I believe in "*Down to Earth*" behavior with an "*Skyward Bound*" attitude.

Let's apply this concept in the context of social media. Social media is fooling you & channeling you to work free for them, making money out of your time. Be smart! Don't get fooled by social media. Understand your time-worth & do some worthy things.

22.32 Every Minute Count & It's Always High Time!

Life is always short, time is always high & there is always long way to go...

Life is short! Why waste even a second of it? Isn't it a better idea to cut the time on useless activities & invest the saved time in activities that give real happiness? If every second wasted on social media can be saved, it will quickly add up to save hundreds of hours. You can use that time to pursue your passions & make your life worthier & happy! To sum it up:

- *Because life is short*, don't waste it
- *Because time is always high*, act right now
- *Because there is always long way to go*, don't regret, just move on. You can still make it!

22.33 Remember: It's Never Too Late!

I think, by now, you know very well, the difference between offline social life & online social life. While the former makes you happy, the latter can damage your happiness and make you unhappy. Social Media Abuse might have damaged much time in your life, but it's not too late & it's never too late. All of us still have a lot of our life. Let's make it better now with real social-life!

22.34 Be Ethical!

Many People forget how to communicate when it comes to social media, their ethics are gone & they are different person when talk online. They use all kinds of words online even when they can't speak those words in their offline life. Online abuse has become a normal phenomenon now. Be it Prime Minister or President of a country, a political or sports personality or just a common person expressing views, people are abusing everybody, using their fake profiles &

uncivilized language. Is it ethical? Is this what we call a civilized society?

Again, I'm most worried about children here. Children are the most vulnerable audience in the online world. They don't know what's right or wrong and what happens online has a huge-huge impact on their mentality. After all, the content we consume impact us in every way. So, we need to stay ethical, stay respectful: online as well offline! That's the role we can play to make world a better place. And yeah... when such individual contribution becomes a community contribution, the impact is huge! So, Be Ethical!

22.35 Either Ignore It or Take It Seriously!

Social Media Abuse is not considered as serious as offline abuse. We need to make it clear that abuse is abuse: online or offline doesn't make a difference. Online abuse also hurt feelings the same way as offline abuse. I would like to discuss here my personal experience here...

Like just another day, I was checking my Inbox for new mails when I noticed a mail from some unknown person. That email was sent using contact form of my personal website VishnuGoyal.com. In the email, that person had used very harsh language telling me that my website is illegal & s/he will complain about it! In the signature field, my name was used. When I tried to respond, I found that in the "email field" of the contact form, my own email-ID Vishnu@VishnuGoyal.com was used...

... The incidence didn't surprise me at all as I hear cases about all kinds of online abuse & spam. I don't know what kind of fun people make out of it. Anyway, the only way to track that person was IP address which is a cumbersome process and I didn't go for it. The incidence is more than 8 months old at the time of writing this book. I ignored it because there was nothing serious in that email & I know my website is legal. Telling me that it's illegal is just a bad joke! Further, the person didn't mention any information except what is mentioned on my personal website coupled with some harsh language! So, I ignored it...

... What would you do in the same situation? Well, I think if it's a minor & one-time issue (like I got that spam email), it's better to ignore. But if someone is constantly sending messages/emails or abusing you via other kind of media, you should definitely take it seriously & take the appropriate action. Don't ignore such things considering it "*just another online issue*".

22.36 Small Take on Your Beloved "Loud(y) Music"

Today music communities like *SoundCloud* are there! It's great for music lovers! Although, music doesn't form part of typical social media, music is an important part of your *digital-lifestyle*! So, I decided to briefly discuss concern about "*too much & too loudly*" music.

World Health Organization ("*WHO*") has found that about 110 crores teenagers and adults are in danger of hearing loss due to unsafe use of music devices. Nearly 50% people in age group of 12-35 years, living in middle & high-income countries, listen to music at a very high volume and 40% are exposed to dangerous levels of music at clubs, bars & other sports events. To shock you further, would like to quote that 430 lacs people in the age-group of 12-35 years have already lost their hearing ability due to music. You definitely don't want to be included in this number. So, *PLAY IT SAFE!*[111]

22.36 Finally, You Don't Have to Walk on Water!

"Quitting or cutting social media is neither a cake-walk, nor a walk on water"

I would like to tell you my final tip! Controlling your social media and internet habits is not a Walk on water! You can do it! It's all in your hands.

Remember one thing: Social Media is the creation of human beings. Any creature can't be more powerful than its creator. Social media, games, internet, phones, & all these things were created by human beings and being a human being yourself, you are more powerful than social media, internet or any gadgets. You can control it, it can't control you as long as you don't allow it to. So, be your own *Social Media Boss*! And yeah... once again... you don't have to walk on water...!

23.0 Calm Social Media – A Network Specific Perspective

Social Media Networks: There Are Many!

How many social media networks do you use? Don't tell me one! As I know that's a lie! Am I right? Well, you don't need to answer that one too. As I know, I'm right in my prediction! Like many others, probably you are using Facebook, Twitter, WhatsApp, Messenger, Instagram, Tumblr, Pinterest, Snapchat, LinkedIn, WeChat, et cetera, et cetera, et cetera!

As per recent US Android data reports of "*SimilarWeb*" (a Market Intelligence Service company), on average, Facebook user spent 58 minutes in the app, Instagram user spent 53 minutes in the app, Snapchat user spent 49.5 minutes in the app.[112] I decided to cover dedicated tips for each of these platforms (except Snapchat) to calm it! Let's start!

24.0 Calm Facebook

With over 220+ crore users, Facebook is the biggest social media network. Today a person who is not on Facebook is considered as *Anti-social*. Well, I don't think so.

Considering Facebook spams, I support the statement that "*Facebook is an Anti-social Media*".[113] Well, I will not dig deeper into that part as that's another debate and we are here to Calm Social Media.

As per survey held after *Facebook Cambridge Analytica Scandal* (in which personal data of more than 87 million[114] Facebook users was misused for improper political gains), "*just*" 6%[115] of Facebook users are going to permanently delete their Facebook account. It shows how emotionally connected people are to Facebook! People are sacrificing their security, privacy, personal data & everything that Facebook knows about them (which is a lot!) just for the sake of being on Facebook.

Literally, people have become a puppet of Facebook's like, share & comment game! Well, I don't want to offence anybody, but it's important that truth be told. Anyway, we are here to discuss how can we quit/ cut Facebook from our life. Let's proceed...

24.1 Facebook Alarming Stats

Before calming Facebook, let's explore what happens on Facebook in a minute[116]:

- About 300 new profiles are created (5 new profiles per second)
- About 208,333 photos are uploaded (300 million photo uploads per day)
- About 510,000 comments are posted
- About 293,000 users update their status
- 3,298,611 posts are shared (4.75 billion posts are shared on Facebook each day!)

If you are using Facebook just for time-pass, these stats are alarming, and given that, you must think about what you do on Facebook!

24.2 More Facebook = More Negativity & Stress

On average, 220+ crore Facebook users spend (or waste) about 35 minutes a day on Facebook. Time you spend on Facebook leads to greater anxiety, anxiety disorders, increase in stress & negative feelings. People who quit Facebook are happier ones! So, quitting Facebook is the best option you can opt for to simplify your social media life. If you can't quit Facebook, at least cut time you spent on it before you need "*Facebook pills or drugs*" to deal with your Facebook addiction!

24.3 Facebook & Your Well-Being – The Relationship

Let's keep it short: Quitting Facebook leads to higher levels of well-being. Yes. Facebook impacts your well-being negatively. Study[117] found that:

> *"break from Facebook has positive effects on the two dimensions of well-being: our life satisfaction increases, and our emotions become more positive"*

Well, if you use Facebook just for personal use, I am in favor of quitting Facebook. Just delete it. It's one of the best decisions you can take to simplify your life & be happier.

24.4 The Story of Likes

Right from when the Facebook like button was invented, it has been copied by all the social media platforms in one form or the another. Twitter, Instagram, Tumblr & other apps' "*heart-shaped-likes*" are good examples here! While more likes than expected may make you feel good but getting lower than expected create a feeling of non-fulfilment & dissatisfaction. It can make you feel yourself of a loser. It's a "*Like-Trap*" & to get yourself out of this business of "*keeping you hooked*", you need a determination, a strong one. Well, in later sections, we'll discuss how to outsmart Facebook before it outsmarts you.

24.5 Let's Play Facebook Q&A

To calm Facebook & to understand how much good or bad friend Facebook is for you, ask these questions to yourself:

- How many times you visit Facebook App just to read some useless notifications?
- How many friends you have on Facebook (I guess hundreds or thousands!). Are all of them your actual friends?
- How much do you care about your Facebook friends? (Well that a question you need to ask from yourself but notifications from these so-called friends doesn't care about your time at all. These eat up your time so quickly!)
- Why you often find yourself scrolling through your Facebook feed?
- How many times a day do you check your Facebook account?
- How often you pick-up your phone to check how many likes, shares & comments your recent post has got?
- Do you feel compel to check your Facebook?

Did you answer those questions? Yep! Well, by now, you must have realized that you waste a lot of your time on Facebook. Sometimes, it just makes me feel that people are not using Facebook, Facebook is using people. Fortunately, there are many cures to Facebook Problem. Let's explore them...

24.6 Facebook Prescription!

I have got some practical tips to cut the time you spend on Facebook. Here we go:

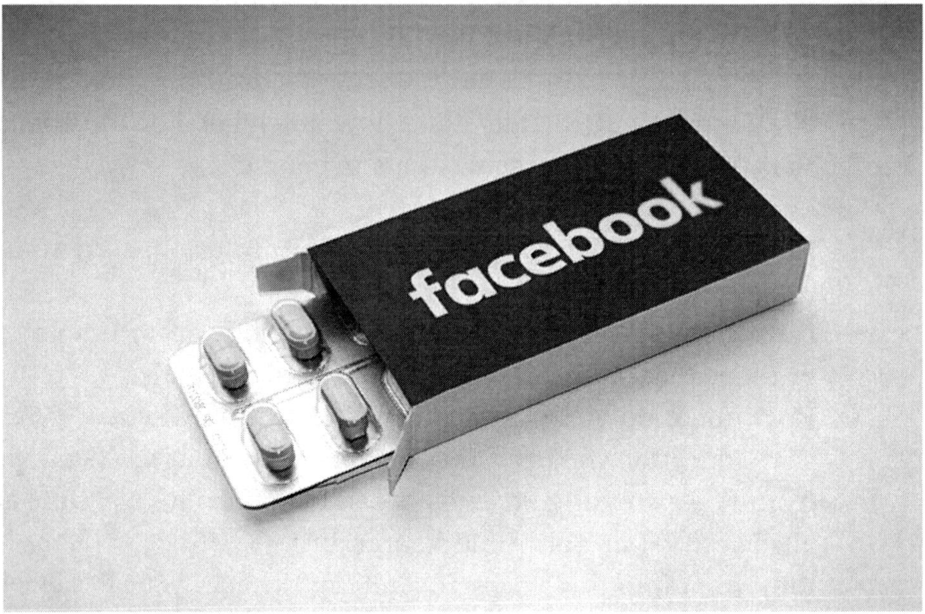

[Illustration by *Media Modifier*[118] at *Pixabay*]

- *Unfriend the friends who are not your friends actually!*
  You know what I'm talking about. So, don't ask for more. It will reduce the number of posts you get in your feed, which will result in less time you spend in the feed.

- *Unlike pages you don't care about.*
  You liked a page 5 year ago but now you no longer interested in it & you're still getting updates from such page in your feed. Why don't you unlike it. Do that & do that for all such pages.

- *Limit who can send you friend requests.*
  By default, everybody & anybody can send you a friend request! Perhaps you never changed those settings & that's why you keep getting tens or hundreds or thousands of

friends requests each day. Fortunately, Facebook has built-in setting allowing you to change the "*Who can send you friend requests?*" option from "*Everyone*" to "*Friends of Friends*".

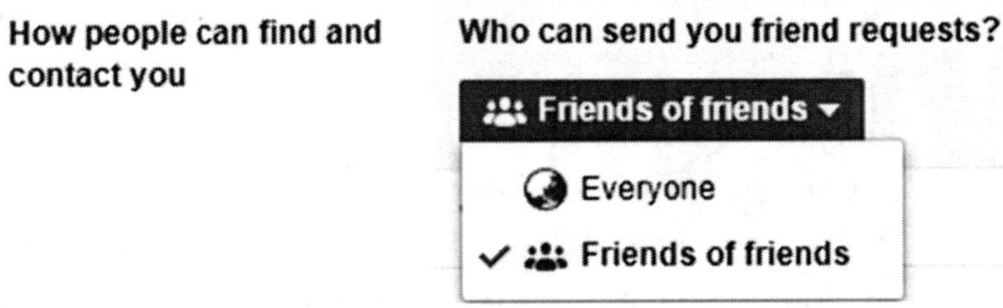

[Facebook Settings - Who Can Send You Friend Requests?]

Feel free to opt for it. This way you can reduce friend requests from unknown people. Result will be less requests, less notifications & less time spend on clicking that "*Ignore*" button!

- *Hide Your Email & Phone Number.*
  By default, anyone with your email ID & phone number can look up for your profile. Apart from Facebook, family & friends, you give your phone number & email ID to many people & some of them may have wrong intentions about you. Such bad guys can be tracking you on social media & make you a target of Social Media Abuse & bullying. You don't want to help such guys, right? So, go to Facebook privacy settings & hide your email & phone number from public look-up. This way, people will not be able to find you by your phone number or email-ID. A better, smart & safe approach, right?

- *Control Who Can See Your Posts.*
  Since Facebook wants its users to spend more & more time on the platform, by default, everyone on Facebook can see your

posts. You can customize this setting & choose who can see your posts. Just go to Facebook privacy settings & set "*Who can see your future posts*" option to:

- ✓ "*Friends*" (which, perhaps the best option available. You can also ban annoying *friend* or *friends* with "*friends except...*" option), or
- ✓ "*some specific friends*" or
- ✓ "*only me*" (I think no one would select "*only me*" option as no one share posts on Facebook just for one self!).

Have a look at this snapshot from Facebook settings menu for a visual grasp of this option:

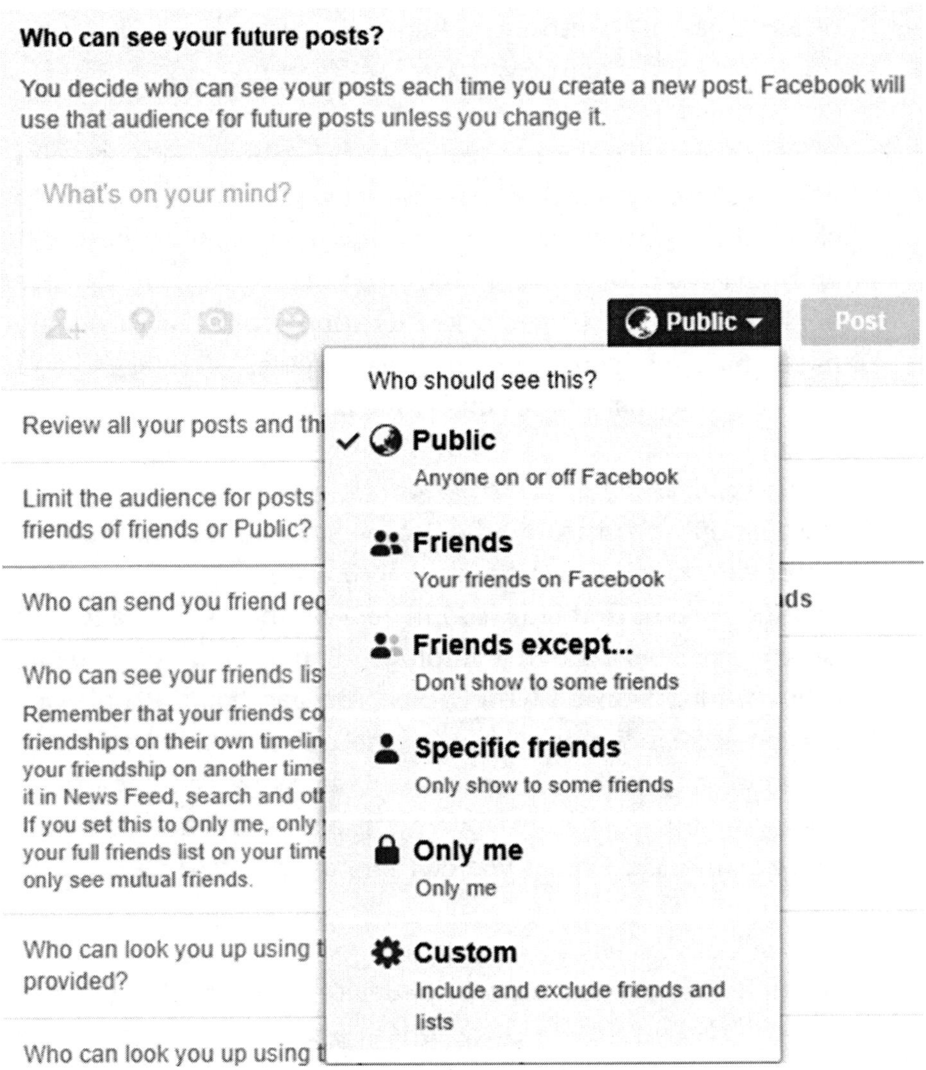

[Facebook Settings - Who Can See Your Future Posts]

By exercising this option, you can protect yourself from getting abused by unknown or anonymous people with fake profiles. Saves lot of trouble & time as well! To explore other settings, go to Facebook.com/settings. There you can find other useful settings like "*Location*", "*Blocking*", "*Notifications*", "*Apps & websites*", et cetera...

... While you might be aware of such settings, but these are often ignored given the busy schedule, right? Feel free to check these options & customize them as per your needs. It will save you lots of time & trouble in long run. On my personal profile, I have blocked location access for Facebook, have blocked some inappropriate users & pages and subscribed to just important notifications!

- *My Best Suggestion – "Just Delete It".*
  My best tip is to uninstall the Facebook app from your gadget. Don't worry. You can check the Facebook in your browser, but you'll get rid of that blue icon in your phone. You'll no longer see the Facebook icon in your phone. Believe it or not, it'll has a huge impact on how much you use Facebook. People use Facebook for few minutes to few hours on a daily basis. You are among them too. I assure you, removing Facebook from your phone will free up your brain and will leave you with more quality time to let you do more of what you really love.

- *Turn off notifications.*
  If you don't have the courage to delete Facebook, no worries. You can still turn off notifications at least. It will help you cut some distractions from your life & be more productive. After all, most of the Facebook notifications are worthless.

- *Be inspired from people who've already done it!*
  I don't want to appreciate myself here, but it's necessary that experience which can help you Calm Social Media, be told. I deleted Facebook from my phone months ago & it's one of the

best decisions I have ever taken. Now, I do check it occasionally in browser. Probably once in 15 days & that too for maximum 5 minutes. But since I'm in online business, I need to post more often & for that I use some other tools but not Facebook!

To further inspire you, let me shock you with this: ***Justin Rosenstein, Creator of Facebook Like Button removed Facebook from his phone over addiction fears***![119]

I would also like to let you know about Britt![120] Britt writes at *TinyAmbitions.com* & she made a similar move (I mean deleting Facebook) to *Calm Facebook*. She crowned her decision as "*The Best thing I've Done To Simplify My 'Social' Life*". Well, I think that all people say similar words after deleting Facebook subject to the condition that they have the will-power to do so & remain stick to their decision. Britt rightly stated: "*You may love cat videos but scrolling through Facebook for hours to watch them is not a good use of your time!*"

- *Be a part of initiative. Be Smart.*
  Negative effects of Facebook like peer pressure, stress, Facebook addiction, fake news, FOMO[121], time waste, threat to democracy, its anti-social nature[122] and much more, seems to outweigh Facebook's benefits. Do you think it's worth your valuable time? Well, I don't think so. That's what Calm Social Media initiative is all about. So, be a part of Calm Social Media initiative to make social media a better place!

- *Be Aware of Your Friend List.*
  I have seen profiles on Facebook with "*incredibly stupid friend list*" that may run in thousands of friends (I'm sure you too

must have come across such incredibly ridiculous social profiles. Haven't you?). I mean are they really friends? We all have just 1,440 minutes in a day & if we have our friends number running in thousands, we don't have even a minute for each one of them! It is certain that these so called "*online-friends*" will not add any value to your life, but posts from such "*fake-friends*" landing in your newsfeed will certainly help you in killing your time and being a *social media puppet* (I'm not sorry for my language! I need to use these words to make people on wrong path realize the right thing! No offence!)

Well, that's how you can Calm Facebook. I think you've got sufficient Facebook medication! Let's proceed to Calm Instagram now...

25.0 Calm Instagram

25.1 Most Worst, Most Negative, Most Dangerous & Detrimental of All!

Before delving into "*Calm Instagram*", let me shock you! Of all social media apps, Instagram has the most worst, most negative & detrimental effect on your mental health.[123] Selfies meant for Instagram has led to death of many people & a new term has emerged called "*Selfie-Death*". While it is bitter to hear, but I believe that Instagram is the "*largest place of fakeness*" in the online world where everyone seems to be happy & living a 5-star life!

On Instagram, you post & see variety of photos, but most of the times you post & see selfies, right? Well, among all media, selfie has proved to be the most dangerous thing. Due to their personal nature, when you capture selfies, your entire focus is shifted on the camera lens & you become unaware about what's going on around you.

For many people, posting new photos, waiting for likes & comments on them & deleting it, if it doesn't get "*enough*" likes, is a common phenomenon! What's the result? Result is, time waste in capturing photos, editing & posting it, anxiety to frequently check your Instagram & see how many comments & like your post has got and depression, feeling of un-fulfilment & inferiority on not getting enough likes. Does it happen with you? You don't need to tell me or the world about it. Just ask it from yourself & get the answer.

Escape from all this is simple: just delete Instagram & keep your memories with you in your private cloud where you don't crave for likes & comments! I have already said it many times: the net effect of using social media for personal purpose is negative! Leave the brands, businesses & celebrities aside. They are using social media as part of their work. Their case is different.

25.2 Instagram Safety Prescription

Let's Calm Instagram & "*Be Safe*" with these Instagram safety measures:

- *Selfie Safety*
  Reportedly, in 2015 alone, selfie took life of at least 27 people & at least 50% of such deaths occurred in India.[124] Such reports demand that you need to take care of your "*selfie habits*". People take selfie while driving, on escalators, in lifts, in malls, on airports, in metro & everywhere else! We must understand that each place is not suitable to take a selfie. Senseless selfie can cost our lives. We may fall from stairs, fall in a running metro, loose our senses of what's going on around us (as when you're busy taking selfie, your mind focus is shifted on your camera) & there are several other reasons as well. Take selfie. but take it safe!

"Take selfie. but take it safe!"

Is liking that bloody Instagram photo of a dog or a cat is really important than talking to the person sitting with you or taking a good night's sleep. I don't think it is. But I leave it to you. Because if you are wise enough to invest your precious time in reading this book, you are surely wise enough to have the right answer to my question.

- Don't Capture! Just Live!
  Today we rarely find people with a phone without a camera! No matter whether the person is smart or not, but the phone must be smart!

  Be it birthday, wedding, travelling, casual parties or other celebrations, you don't live any moment anymore. you just want to digitize those moments with your camera!

  Think about it - how mad thing is that! You are not enjoying the moments when they are with you & later you keep scrolling through these moments in your photo library, Facebook & Instagram feed. So, the best way to enjoy those moments to the fullest is: *Don't capture. Just live!*

- *"No Selfie" doesn't Mean That You Are Missing Out!*
  In the Instagram world, people who don't do silly things like taking selfie everywhere, selfies with some bizarre facial expressions, are considered as "*outdated*", "*boring*", "*fools*" and blah, blah, blah! I have personally experienced this, as I am not a "*selfie guy*"! Till date, I don't have a single selfie & I don't plan to have one in future. That doesn't mean that me

or others like me, who are not interested in selfies are a tech-fool.

I pity for people whose instinct beg for a selfie every few hours (every few minutes in a case of few people). Such people don't know what they are missing out by keeping themselves busy in capturing every moment of their life. They are not living, they are *just capturing*. "*True Living*" is what "*Selfie People*" are missing out. So, "*No Selfie*" doesn't mean that you're missing out. In fact, "*Selfie*" means that you're missing out.

26.0 Social Media & Parenting

While we have already discussed "*Gaming, Children & Parenting: Wake-up Call*" in earlier sections, but I've got more to talk about this!

Though I am not a parent, but fortunately I do have three nieces & I love them all! Whenever I see them, most of the times I found them busy with their parents' smartphone & sometimes they catch mine! (They don't have their own as one is just 2 years old, other is 3 & the eldest one is 5. Children of such age don't deserve their own smartphone. It's a sad thing that some people don't understand this small thing). Though they don't have their own social media accounts but still they're online for the most of their "*free time*", either watching videos on YouTube or playing random games. Whenever I notice their digital activity, I feel worried about their online behavior & for their online safety. We all know that there is lots of content on YouTube which is not appropriate for children. Further, hours of screen time can be unhealthy for them...

... I decided to take an action. I installed YouTube kids in the smartphones they use (thanks to Google for dedicated app for kids) which is much safer for children & contain child-friendly videos. I also asked my sisters to uninstall "*addictive games*" from their smartphones & keep an eye on what they do online and put a check on their screen time. It would be much better if they engage in physical gaming activities then spending time on playing *Candy*

Crush. And yeah... for children, there are better and educational games available. Why shouldn't we install them & let them play those ones?

If you have children, you've also got an extra job! Don't worry. It's about simple parenting and I'm not asking for an interrogation. I'm just asking you to take care of what your children are doing with your or their gadgets as what they do today, has huge impact on their future. Kids have "*little-to-no sense*" of right or wrong & it's where you have a role to play – guiding them properly & monitoring their online behavior. Their restricted use of social media & smartphone may make them feel bad & at times, they may be angry with you, but it's worth for their long-term prosperity. If they have their own smartphones, your job become even more serious!

As per *Australian Psychology Society*, 60% of the parents never monitor their children's social media accounts.[125] That's alarming! Monitoring children's online activities should be an important part of parenting. You must be connected to your child's online world. Be a part of it. It will also put a moral check on your children.

"All Parents – Be Proactive"

Today, children online are facing problems like cyber-bullying, abusive messages & emails, inappropriate video content, communication with unknown people & lots of other issues. In these situation, as a parent, your support will be invaluable. Children rarely talk about these issues to their parents, but you can be proactive. Take right steps at the right time to save your children from the social media & online danger. Before they grow up enough to understand the difference of right or wrong, you should be an inseparable part of their online journey. Well, that's my thoughts. Of course, I am no body to tell you what you should or shouldn't do as a parent or guardian. But I also think that if my words can have a positive impact on even a single life, I should spread them all! For sure, final action lies on you.

27.0 Email – How to Use It Better?

Although email is very different thing than that social media, but I think in some ways it is related to social media. So, I decided to take a quick & brief tour of few email problems & solutions in a "*very-lite-mode*". Don't expect much on it, at least for now! Let's do it...

27.1 Email overload

Email is an indelible part of our work-life balance as well as imbalance! It's balance for those who know how to manage it, while for others Inbox is a total mess!

If you are checking your Inbox every few minutes, it's simply an indication of how hard-working-non-smart type of person you are. If you want to accomplish some real work, it requires focused approach. Why can't you fix some intervals in between your email check-ups, for like 1 hour or 2 hours? I mean you can check your inbox at a frequency of 1 hour or 2 hours or any other time-interval, as you think, would be appropriate for you. I don't think that any email is so urgent that it needs to be replied immediately. I know that some people will argue about this. Okay! Okay! I got you...

... Exceptions might be there. If that extraordinary email is so urgent, the sender should be mindful enough to have a call with you, informing the urgency. In case s/he doesn't, that's not your fault. (Okay. No more arguments on this. After all we are not here to debate about email etiquettes). Let's stop the arguments before it gets heated & discuss some email stats followed by some email tricks:

27.2 Email Facts & Stats

Before going for simplifying your inbox & lighten your email pressure, let's enlist some of the most surprising, fun, & useful email stats for better understanding:

- 49.7% of the total emails are considered as spam and USA, Russia & China are top spam producing countries
- 35% of the marketing emails are opened solely on the basis of its subject line
- 17% of email users in America change their email ID every 6 months
- 30% of email users change their email ID every year
- 35% of the professionals use email on their mobile devices
- People under 25 years old prefer messaging over email
- By 2019 start, there will be 380 crore email users in the world & the number is expected to grow to 420 crores by 2022
- On average, each user has 1.75 email IDs
- Each day, average professional receives 121 emails & sends out 40
- iPhone is the most popular device for checking emails
- On Tuesday, more emails are opened than any other day of the week (so send important emails on Tuesday!)

Well, the "*estimated fact*" that by 2019, there will be 380 crore people using email & the number is expected to grow to 420 crores by 2022, is great. It represents that more & more people are joining the online world. Further, the fact that average user has 1.75 e-IDs gives a hint on how much fake accounts are there in the online world. Though few people may be having different IDs for personal & business use, but I still think that governments should regulate the online world more strictly and all email addresses & social profiles should be linked to "*Legal-Digital-Identity*" (going to discuss it shortly!).

27.3 Simple Email Tricks

- *Do Weekly Email Check-up*
  Sometimes, we just subscribe to some websites we don't need & at other times, websites hack our email IDs to get us subscribed, without us even knowing about the subscription! Weekly email-check-up is the solution you should consider. It means clean-up your Inbox at least once in a week. Unsubscribe from updates you are no longer interested in & don't leave any unread email. It will help you stop the *Complied Burdon* of thousands of unread emails on your head and you'll not get those unwanted updates from the unsubscribed sources. Result will be: *Less emails, clean inbox & more productive time*!

- *Don't check your email too frequently*
  If you have email-disorder of checking your email every few minutes, I think you need to take care of your habit! I know

some work-related & other emails may be urgent & need to be answered immediately, but even during work hours, you should fix a gap of at least an hour to check your Inbox.

- *Take Care of When & Where You Check It!*
  Few people keep checking their Inbox, no matter what the time is, no matter where they are! Whether they are at home or in office, be it morning, evening or night, they have their inbox screen open all the time! Not right!

  Our mind is not a machine & it needs rest too. You should endeavor to make sure that you don't have to check your Inbox in the evening or at night too often (I know it's unavoidable, that's why I'm saying too often!).

- *Not mentioned here...*
  As I said already, we will have a limited discussion on "*email usage*" in this book & we just had it! There are lots of other email tricks as well that are not mentioned here, as we've got much more to talk about Social Media Abuse & we've limited time. No worries! If you want me to write more about it, do let me know, I'll do it on CalmSocialMedia.com. Okay? Yep!

28.0 One Tough Question: Can Social Media Companies Be Held Liable for Social Media Abuse?

28.1 My Answer

No, is my answer.

The job of social media companies is to make & design their website or app in a way that can attract more and more visitors. They want to retain you with their best "*user experience*" as they call it. They are doing their job quite well. They also consider themselves playing important role in connecting people and giving people the power to freely express themselves. I appreciate such good intention.

28.2 Who Is at Fault?

I was wrong in using (exploiting) social media. You are wrong in harassing social media. We are wrong! You are addicted to it and you need to be changed, not the social media.

28.3 "Who Is Culprit" Illustration

Let's know "who is at fault?" with an illustration...

... There are sleeping pills available in the market which are primarily used to induce sleep and in the treatment of sleeplessness (called insomnia!). So, intention behind invention of sleeping pills was good. The companies making sleeping pills have no intention to murder/ kill anybody. However, we see cases of people who took excessive sleeping pills and lost their life...

... Here I need to ask one ridiculous, yet very important question:

"Can Sleeping pills or the pharmaceutical company making such pills be held responsible for the death of the people who had the overdose?"

Obviously no!

I leave the rest of the inference up to you. You are wise enough to judge who is at fault: Social Media or the Social Media Addict (You)?

29.0 My Take on Digital Well-being Initiatives of Tech Giants

With great user-base, comes a great responsibility! Tech-Giant companies like Google, Facebook, Instagram, Apple, Amazon, WhatsApp, Twitter & many others have crores of people using their services. I think that these companies are responsible to investigate how their products or services affect the lives of the users of their products or services. If it is noticed that their users are affected negatively with their offerings, these companies should be proactive in their actions to prevent the damage to their users. While some companies are working for the well-being of their users, others exist just for the sake of money! Let's explore a few aspects in this direction & know what tech-giants are up-to!

Firstly, I would like to talk about Google. As far as my knowledge is concerned, Google is the most proactive company working towards the Digital well-being! Thankfully Google has "*initiated an initiative*" dubbed as "*Google Digital Wellbeing*" to make people "*internet-smart*".[126]

YouTube's new "*take-break-reminder*" feature is part of Google's focus to make you aware about how much time you spend on YouTube & to help you limit your YouTube time. You can choose to receive this take-break reminder at a frequency customized by you!

This way YouTube can help you spend less time on YouTube as you will be getting reminder to take a break from your YouTube watch time!

I wish Facebook could bring a similar feature especially for those who are addicted to the social media giant's addictive service! Well, I don't think we can see it till Facebook leadership comes in hands of some better people.

Anyway, YouTube's take-break notification is a good move as once we turn to YouTube, we don't know how 5 minutes turned to an hour or more of continuous watching supported by auto-play of the next video & video suggestions based on our search & watch history (Google knows us well!).

Unlike *Facebook* & "*most other companies*", *Google* seemed to be a people-friendly company & I have no hesitation in saying that. I have experienced Facebook as a personal user as well as a business user. To me, Facebook is a company focused solely on money, given the fact that it works with growth-at-all-costs mentality.[127] It shows repeated notifications, show over-personalized ads[128], falsely collects users' personal data at the back of its terms & conditions[129] which are just impossible to understand for many of its users, sell[130] users' data with so-called users' permission – permission users don't even know about and when damage is done, offers an apology that can't rectify anything retrospectively.[131]

People who are using Facebook for personal interest are making a fool of themselves.

I believe that Google is really working to make the web a better place & help people live a better digital life. YouTube "*Notification*

Digest" feature which let you choose to get YouTube notifications as a daily digest, instead of a new notification every time a channel you are subscribed to publishes a video, is a commendable move to reduce the number of notification you get on your smartphone! Once again, an initiative that suggests that Google cares about people. Further, "*Be Internet Awesome*"[132] & "*YouTube Kids*" [133] by Google are a few examples of Google initiatives to ensure digital safety of children.

Further, Google's "*Android P*" version will tackle the smartphone addiction problem. The new version of android will introduce a new feature called "*Android Dashboard*"[134] which will help you track your smartphone usage. You'll be able to see how much time you spend on your phone & on what apps! Interesting & useful, right? But wait! Why a tech company like Google wants to make you aware about your smartphone usage & help you put it down? I think the answer to this question is: *Responsible Corporate Citizen*! Chasing money should not be the only objective of any company. It's the responsibility of any ethical & responsible company to make sure that its products & services doesn't harm the well-being of its customers or users. I think Google knows it well & it's a responsible corporate citizen! That's why it's taking all these efforts without any regulatory pressure (was thinking about Facebook here!), even though it may cost its profits!

Given the addictive nature[135] of its devices, Apple has also introduced it's "*Digital Wellbeing*" app called "*Screen Time*"[136], which will be available in iOS 12. The new app has features which are quite similar to "*Android Dashboard*" features we just discussed. To maintain brevity, I will not go into details of the app here, but yes, I would like to add one thing: With "*Screen Time*", Apple's purpose is to make you aware about *how* you spend your time on your phone & to help you cut your screen time, which is the need of tech-stressed life. Reportedly, the new iOS will focus on digital well-being with features like group notifications to reduce the number of distractions, an improved "*do-not-disturb*" mode, et cetera. Great efforts from Apple! Well done!

I'm sure that once you are aware about how much time you waste on your phone & social media, you'll take steps to restrict your use & will spend more time in real life. You'll feel the "*JOMO*" i.e. the "*Joy of Missing Out*" as Google's *Sundar Pichai* dubbed it to explain his idea of unplugging.[137].

While such kind of initiatives are not expected yet from Facebook & Instagram given their leadership so far, it will be ethical & fruitful if other tech companies take inspiration from Google & Apple for digital well-being of their users & try to make their services less addictive with *not-so-good* user experience!

30.0 Thoughts, Opinions, Analysis & Advice from Few Big Names & Brands

30.1 Tim Martin, Chairman, Wetherspoons

Wetherspoons, a famous pub company in the United Kingdom & Ireland, closed all Facebook. Twitter, Instagram & other social media accounts for its individual pubs and its chairman, Mr. Martin said[138]:

> *"We are going against conventional wisdom that these platforms are a vital component of a successful business... We were also concerned that pub managers were being side-tracked from the real job of serving customers... if people limited their social media to half an hour a day, they'd be mentally and physically better off"*
>
> *"society would be better off if people cut the amount of social media use"*

It may be inferred from the above statements that social media profiles of *Wetherespoons* were distracting its managers from their job of serving customers which means social media is distracting and can severely affect your job. Further, Tim Martin's statement suggest that the more you limit your social media use, the more better life you lead.

30.2 Mozilla

After Facebook's Cambridge Analytica Scandal (wherein up to 87 million Facebook users[139], a figure much higher than initially reported figure of 50 million users[140], had their information used by Cambridge Analytica, a private company, without their knowledge or consent), Mozilla (the organization behind Firefox, which works on the principle of "*Internet for people, not profit*") temporarily stopped advertising on Facebook & I would like to quote the excerpt from its statements on the matter:

> *"Facebook knows a great deal about their two billion users — perhaps more intimate information than any other company does. They know everything we click and like on their site, and know who our closest friends and relationships are...... we found that its current default settings leave access open to a lot of data – particularly with respect to settings for third party apps..."*[141]
>
> *"Facebook's current app permissions leave billions of its users vulnerable without knowing it...... The default permissions that Facebook gives to those third parties currently include data from your education and work, current city and posts on your timeline...... We're pushing Facebook to improve its privacy practices not just because of its 2 billion users, but also for the health of the internet broadly."*[142]

Mozilla's statement supports the opinion that Facebook (by default) provides third party access to our data without us even knowing about it. Data abuse of 87 million users, coupled with 10+ public apologies[143], also suggest that Facebook cares about its users but only in statements & not in reality. Considering the Mozilla's statement, it would not be wrong to say that, currently, Facebook is a threat to internet health & all Facebook users are sharing their data on the risk of vulnerability & abuse.

30.3 Brian Acton, WhatsApp Co-Founder

Lately, WhatsApp co-founder Brian Acton tweeted[144], "*It is time #deletefacebook*", to tell the world that it's time to delete Facebook! Have a look at his tweet:

[WhatsApp co-founder Brian Acton Tweeted - Delete Facebook]

30.4 Justin Rosenstein, Creator of Facebook Like Button

Justin Rosenstein is the person who invented Facebook's like button, lead its development at Facebook & co-founded Asana (one of the best team-collaboration software & I use it too!). In a statement to Guardian, Rosenstein said (with reference to Facebook):

> *"It is very common...for humans to develop things with the best of intentions and for them to have unintended, negative consequences."*

With reference to social media, he said that[145]:

> *"Everyone is distracted. All of the time."*

Further, as a step to Calm Social Media, Rosenstein has blocked Reddit from his laptop, banned himself from Snapchat & most importantly, has removed the Facebook from his phone. I don't think we can get an inspiration for Calm Social Media better than Justin Rosenstein.

30.5 Yoweri Museveni, President of Uganda

> *"idle talk on social media is costing the country much-needed time & income"*

30.6 Shirley Cramer, Chief Executive of Royal Society for Public Health (RSPH)

> *"Social media has been described as more addictive than cigarettes and alcohol and is now so entrenched in the lives of young people that it is no longer possible to ignore it when talking about young people's mental health issues. It's interesting to see Instagram and Snapchat ranking as the worst for mental health and wellbeing – both platforms are very image-focused, and it appears they may be driving feelings of inadequacy and anxiety in young people."* [146]

30.7 Nir Eyal, Author of "*Hooked: How to Build Habit-Forming Products*"

> *"The technologies we use have turned into compulsions, if not full-fledged addictions...... It's the impulse to check a message notification. It's the pull to visit YouTube, Facebook, or Twitter for just a few minutes, only to find yourself still tapping and scrolling an hour later...... None of this is an accident...... It is all just as their designers intended."*[147]

30.8 Sean Parker, First President of Facebook

Expressing his concern over Facebook negativity, Sean Parker said:

> *"it's exploiting a vulnerability in human psychology...... It literally changes your relationship with society, with each other. It probably interferes with productivity in weird ways. God only knows what it's doing to our children's brains."* [148]

30.9 Roger McNamee, Early Facebook Investor

> *"In order to maximize its share of human attention, Facebook employed techniques designed to create an addiction to its platform."*[149]

30.10 Adam Alter, Marketing and Psychology Professor at New York University Stern School of Business

> *"Today, unfortunately, many tech developments do promote addiction."* [150]

30.11 Marc Benioff, CEO of Salesforce

In his statements, Benioff suggested that Social Media should be regulated like a health issue, similar to tobacco and sugar[151]:

> *"I think that you do it exactly the same way that you regulated the cigarette industry. Here's a product: Cigarettes. They're addictive, they're not good for you...... I think that for sure, technology has addictive qualities that we have to address, and that product designers are working to make those products more addictive and we need to rein that back."*

30.12 George Soros, Investor & Philanthropist

In his statement, Soros compared Facebook & Google with Casinos:

> *"they deliberately engineer addiction to the services they provide[152]."*

30.13 Tony Fadell, iPhone Co-creator

> *"Apple Watches, Google Phones, Facebook, Twitter – they've gotten so good at getting us to go for another click, another dopamine hit...... They now have a responsibility & need to start helping us track & manage our digital addictions across all usages – phone, laptop, TV etc."* [153]

30.14 Holly Shakya, Assistant Professor & Social Media Researcher at The University of California

> *"We found that the more you use Facebook over time, the more likely you are to experience negative physical health, negative mental health and negative life satisfaction."* [154]

30.15 Andrew Bosworth, VP, Facebook

Emphasizing the negative side of Facebook's global connectivity, Andrew wrote in a Facebook memo:

> *"Maybe it costs a life by exposing someone to bullies...... Maybe someone dies in a terrorist attack coordinated on our tools."* [155]

30.16 Dr. Helen Driver, Somnologist and Assistant Professor at Queen's University in Kingston

> *"The explosion of social media and people staying on devices for longer – and taking them to bed with them – is a huge problem"* [156]

30.17 Julia Carrie, Technology Reporter, Guardian US

> *"Facebook's great value has come from making the rest of us lose control."* [157]

30.18 David Pierce, Senior Staff Writer at WIRED

> *"You can turn off all the Facebook notifications you don't want (assuming you can figure out how) but Facebook will just invent and opt you into new types."* [158]

30.19 Chamath Palihapitiya, CEO of Social Capital & Former Facebook Sr. Executive

At Stanford Graduate School of Business, Chamath Palihapitiya described Facebook as *shit & a global problem.* He also recommended a break from social media. Here are some important words of wisdom from his interview:

> *"I think we have created tools that are ripping apart the social fabric of how society works...... The short-term, dopamine-driven feedback loops that we have created are destroying how society works. No civil discourse, no cooperation, misinformation, mistruth...... This is a global problem...... I can control my decision, which is that I don't use that shit. I can control my kids' decisions, which is that they're not allowed to use that shit."*[159]

30.20 Jenny Radesky, MD, American Academy of Pediatrics

> *"Families should proactively think about their children's media use and talk with children about it, because too much media use can mean that children don't have enough time during the day to play, study, talk, or sleep."*[160]

Well, we just had a look on some of the worthiest opinions in the world of technology & social media. Mine & your opinion counts too. I would be waiting for you to tell me what you think of the social media & technology in general & how it's effecting your life. Feel free to drop a mail to me anytime. And yeah... speak carefree, not careless. Okay?

31.0 I've Got Homework for You!

I hope by now, you know that social media is not that important or not important at all and you can live without it! But, if you still have doubts, do one experiment. Here are the steps...

I. Make a list of all activities you do on social media (like reading news, sharing photos, mindless scrolling, checking updates from friends & family)

II. Take a note of how much time you spend on social media for a week

III. Suspend social media for a week from your lifestyle, find alternate services or solutions for doing the same activities as you do on social media (like find some news apps for news or just get it via a newspaper in the morning, keep photos in personal cloud & share those via a link with your loved ones, arrange meetups or calls with friends & family members to check what they are up to, et cetera) & take a note of how much time it takes to perform those activities with such other alternatives for a week

IV. Note the time savings (the difference between time noted in step II & step III. Also, feel the difference in your happiness level.

V. Do let me know about your experiment & how do you feel about it.

Once you cross the steps of this awesome experiment, you'll know what you were missing in your life. You'll want to cut your time on social media, trust me! Yeah... the initial 7 days of step 3 of the experiment will be difficult for you, but it will worth the result you'll get! So, be hard on yourself just for 7 days. It can change your life, for good!

One more thing, you can argue that not all social media activities can be carried on with alternatives! Well, I agree. For those, fix a time, say one hour a week. Carry on those activities in one hour (which I think is more than enough) preferably on a decided day of the week so that you don't have to catch up with this nonsense on a daily basis. And yeah... don't forget to set the 50 minutes reminder & a 60 minutes reminder as you know how moments gets converted in hours of scrolling on social media, right? Once the 50 minutes reminder is over, just start wrapping up your social media activities and finally close it immediately once 60 minutes reminder rings, no matter what you are doing on it! This weekly cycle will go on! It will save you hours per week & you'll be happier. Initial days of change may be hard for you as "*new-&-good*" habits take time & pain to develop but think about how much free you feel once you develop them! Once you're able to pass this experiment, you'll feel free from the social media prison. It will be like new independence in your personal life.

32.0 Regulatory Trends in The World of Social Media & Internet

When it to comes to improve the situation of Social Media Abuse & clean the web, people leading Social Media Networks as well as people using Social Media have got a job to do.

People needs to deliberate on how they use social media & their makers need to continuously update the platforms to cater to the ever-rising issues.

I also think that it's where, governments & regulators has a "MAJOR" role to play. Some countries have done much better in this field, some are making new laws, some are thinking about it - after all, trend is different & ongoing all the time!

In this section we'll explore some of the unique solutions that different countries are inventing & implementing to combat the problem of Social Media Abuse and internet & online world in general.

Further, we'll discuss what's more can be done at regulatory level to fight this issue more easily & strongly. Let's explore it together...

32.1 Right to Disconnect

In the online world, we are connected 24/7 (Really, some people attend the calls during sleep hours as well!). That's the reason employees are getting work even after office hours!

No quality time has left for refreshment. The situation has become so worse that one weird, yet highly demanded bill is under consideration in New York that would give its citizens a "*Right to Disconnect*"! [161]

That means it would become illegal for employers in New York to communicate post office hours with their employees regarding work related matters and they shall be penalized for violation![162] So, if you are a New Yorker, you will not need to answer late night work emails, calls & messages & will be able to enjoy quality time and sleep properly! You will have "*Right to Disconnect*"!

Nice law (proposed though)! I would like to see similar laws in all parts of the world, subject to a provision of flexibility for employees, as some people (including me) are nocturnal who prefer to work more at night than day-time. What you think of "*Right to Disconnect*". Feel free to shoot a mail & let me know!

32.2 Social Media Tax

Yeah, you read it right! It's "*Social Media Tax*" i.e. tax on social media services...

... Uganda is planning to tax its social media users! I read about it on Quartz[163] & I want you to know more about it. It's interesting & one of its kind solution to fight Social Media Abuse! Today, lots of people are wasting their precious time on social media sites like Facebook, Twitter, Instagram, Viber & WhatsApp with useless chats & online gossip, spreading fake news & scrolling through their feed again & again. In order to put a check on this malpractice, Uganda is planning a never heard & seen solution – *Tax Social Media Users*! Under the brand new "*Social Media Tax Method*", a daily tax of $0.05 per mobile phone subscriber shall be charged from the people for using social media services. The method is the result of Uganda president's ideology that "*idle talk on social media is costing the country much-needed time & income*". Well, I hope that on roll-out, the new idea will help Uganda to rationalize the social media use in the country & help the country financially as well![164]

Wait! I just said that Uganda is planning tax on social media, right? Well, that's a thing of the past! Tax on social Media in Uganda is in effect now (charged at rate of 200 Ugandan Shillings per user per day[165]). With effect from 1st July 2018, Ugandans have to pay tax for using social media services like Facebook, Twitter, WhatsApp, Skype et cetera. This tax is imposed to regulate the social media use of Ugandans as excessive social media use is costing time & money to the country (& I believe that it's the problem of many countries now). Such tax seeks to curb online gossip & raise government revenue at the same time and can be paid directly through mobile money. I think it will entice Ugandans to cut their time on social media, save time & invest such time in some meaningful activities which will also help in nation's growth & development. Well done Uganda! I wish to see similar initiatives in other countries as well!

Reportedly, Zambia is also planning regulations for "*productive use of internet and social media*" by its people.[166] Considering the social media abuse, I think it will be a great step.

32.3 My Proposed Legal-Digital-Solution to Combat Majority of Online Problems: "*Legal-Digital-Identity*"

As I already stated, there is much more that can be done at legal & regulatory level to bring all kinds of online problems next to zero! Yes, next to zero! I'm talking about a new & prosed solution to make internet & social media clean and I am calling it "***Legal-Digital-Identity***" or "***LDI***". Let's discuss more about it...

.... Today, any person of any age & name can make an email-ID with arbitrary date of birth & name! All of us know what it takes to make ourselves of 18/21 years of age online! Children are the best users of this trick, they take an arbitrary age, make an email-ID & the whole of the online world is open for them. Services which require registration & an age wall, verify you by email-ID & birth date. If you are 18/21 as per your *arbitrary* date of birth, you are so! No legal verification!

Similar kind of situation applies for fake accounts as well. Today, no legal record or verification is required to create an email-ID or social media accounts. Any person can create as many accounts as one wants. That's where the problem of fake accounts lies. I have come across people with more than one Facebook account, more than one Twitter account & so on! Such rascals use their original accounts in civilized manner & use other accounts with fake names for uncivilized purposes like trolling, abusing people, using all kinds of languages, stalking people & the list of "*crimes*" goes on & on...

... What if all the online accounts or the prerequisite thereof (that is email-ID or phone number, which is required to create an online account on any website or app or service) is linked to some sort of legal ID, record & verification? Well, if that is done, there will not be a single fake account, no social media abuse & the web will be a clean place as everyone on the web will be there on legal records as well. No fake accounts...

... Found it overwhelming? I guess, yes! Well, I'm simply saying that If legal verification is there to verify an email address, social media & other type of accounts, Social Media Abuse will drop to perhaps zero level. While the concept of *LDI* can be applied to other online activities as well, here I will limit the talk to Social Media...

... I was saying that if there is some identity which is unique for each person, issued by regulators, and the same is mandatorily linked to all the online accounts of a person, there will be no underage, fake or anonymous profiles. Such ID can be used for legal records & as well as digital records of the people. It will act as legal ID as well as Digital ID of the people. We can simply call it "***Legal-Digital-Identity***" or "***LDI***"! Word "*Legal*" is used before "*Digital*" as firstly, legal verification should be there & then all digital or online accounts of the person should be linked to legal ID. Legal first, digital second as legal things should come first, & then we can allow digital things. Legal first, digital second...

Let's take one example on LDI. In India, we have Aadhar (a 12-digit unique identity number which is mandatorily obtained by residents of India). Aadhar is the unique ID of Indian residents. Indian regulators can make it mandatory to link Aadhar to all online accounts of the Indian residents. Accounts without Aadhar linked to them can be mandatorily suspended. This way, there will be no fake profiles left, people will be accountable for their online activities, no age wall loophole will be there, kids & all people will be safer, no fake news & rumors will be there & internet will be clean!

Based on the above example, regulators can implement the LDI solution in their respective countries. Any accounts without **LDI** linked to them can be mandatorily deleted by social media networks which will make the online world much better...

... Further, some accounts like Facebook, Instagram, Twitter, WhatsApp & Snapchat can be allowed on "***1-4-1***" basis. Means for one *LDI*, only one account will be allowed. Separate permission can be taken for business accounts, if required. This way, only accounts with *LDI* linked to them will be active, others will be deleted within a time frame allotted by the regulators...

... This way, the social media & internet will be much better than it is today. There will be less "*e-crimes*" as today most of the crimes are done with fake & anonymous accounts. Drop in such bogus accounts will also mean a drop in crimes & Social Media Abuse.

Further, if people with real profiles do something wrong, it will be easy for the regulators to know the people behind such profiles (through *LDI* attached to profiles) & quick action can be taken against the wrongdoers. Means, it will be easy to find the culprits & take actions against them. Further, their profiles can be permanently blocked by the regulators with the help of *LDI* termination or suspension and most interestingly, that person will not be able to make a second account due to "1-4-1" concept i.e. only one account is allowed for one *LDI*. Once *LDI* program is in effect, people will think twice before posting anything wrong or involving in Social Media Abuse & "*e-crime*" activities.

Imagine a world where all profiles will be authentic & legally verified! Isn't it a good idea? You can let me know anytime. Further, how should we proceed on this matter to implement this solution deserves a long post. So, will not do it here as I promised, I have kept this book simple, short & non-technical. I'm not going to include legal stuff here.

I hope that I was able to let you take a glimpse into the idea of *LDI*. I know that implementing this will not be a cake-walk, but it will worth the cost & efforts. Want to know more about it & how can we proceed to implement this idea? Well, I think that's for the regulators of the country & the world. But if you want me to elaborate further, do let me know. I'll do posts about *LDI* on CalmSocialMedia.com. Okay? Yep!

33.0 Final Thought: Social Media Is Neither God, Nor Devil. It's Clay!

Yes, Social Media is neither god, nor devil. It's clay!

I consider social media as clay that you can make a god or a devil of. There are many good aspects of social media & there are many bad aspects of social media. which ones you want to pursue, that's up-to you.

Make a heaven or a hell out of it. It totally depends on you.

"Use it less. Use it wisely"

Remember: You should own your social media; your social media should not own you. As long as, you are the boss of your habits, you are good to go. Just keep a check on yourself.

And yeah... I know there are many more aspects of social media and related things that I'm not aware about and so are not included in this book. If you are aware about any such aspects that you feel the world should know, please let me know about it! You can drop your suggestions/ criticism/ advice or any other thoughts at

Vishnu@CalmSocialMedia.com. Everything would we welcome as long as it maintains the dignity.

Further, tech companies are "*Dopamine Dealers*" and just want to please their investors, and not you. These companies use your time to earn for themselves. Every minute you spend on social media (except a few times and moments, which is Okay), you are working for these tech companies without any pay. The people behind these companies are actually destroying you in disguise of providing a platform for connectivity. Operating in disguise of making your life happy, social media is brutally killing you. In the present time, Social Media is no less than a slow poison.

"Social Media is Slow Poison!"

Ab-use of social media, internet, technology harms your creativity, cut the time you spent on work, which badly impact your career in the long run. You as a social media user just remain a puppet of these social media giant companies. It's high time for you and all to understand that social media takes much more from you in comparison to what it gives. Net effect is loss to you.

Finally, I advise you to uninstall the social media apps ASAP. You can use them in your browsers for restricted time, say at a gap of 7 days or 15 days and that too for 15-20 minutes). Don't spend hours. You don't need Facebook or other social media network to read news, connect with your friends or for anything meaningful.

I know that quitting or cutting social media is not a cake walk and it's not a walk on water as well! You can Calm Social Media!

34.0 What's Ahead...

I always thought that this book is not going to be complete ever! And guess what? I was right. Yes. I have published an incomplete book. This book was never complete & will never be. In this edition, I have put all that I could. I know I have not covered all the things, all the topics, all the issues, all the solutions & everything! But, I believe that I have talked about lots of major issues from the world of social media that are impacting our lives & this book will act as an eye-opener for you & all other readers. I believe that it will help you make a new perspective of how you & people around you, see & use social media. I believe that if you have read this book carefully, you will be able to better your social media life, your online life as well as your offline life. Well, that's the thing for now. What's ahead...

... Well, as I just said, this book is incomplete. My research & writing on social media will continue & I will share those in my blog posts on CalmSocialMedia.com. Further, I will be eagerly waiting for your valuable feedback & suggestions on social media & related matters. Also, if at some point of time, I'm convinced that the book needs another edition to cover the further developments & your feedback, I will not wait to come up with an updated edition of Calm Social Media Book.

I am also thinking to build a forum on CalmSocialmedia.com where you'll be able to discuss your social media & related issues and get & give help at the same time. What you think of it? Do let me know!

Also, don't forget to share your Calm Social Media feedback with me.

35.0 Do Me A Favor....

Firstly. Congrats to you! You just completed the Calm Social Media Book! I hope it will lead you towards a better life!

Before, you place this book back to your shelf, I want to ask you for a favor! Just go to amazon website & leave your book review. I will not ask for a 5-star. Leave stars on the scale of 1-5 as you think would fit my work. If you found *Calm Social Media* helpful, please spread the word about it. If you think *Calm Social Media* was a time waste, I'm sorry. Do let me know what was missing. I'll fix it. Okay? Yup!

Thanks for giving your valuable time to read my book!

See you at VishnuGoyal.com & CalmSocialMedia.com!

And yeah...

Do keep moving forward...

References

[1] Tribune.com.pk: Social media 'more addictive than cigarettes and alcohol'.

[2] Reuters.com: Good social media experiences don't outweigh bad ones for young adults.

[3] Rehabs.com: Choosing the Best Internet Addiction Rehab Program.

[4] TheGuardian.com: Does quitting social media make you happier? Yes, say young people doing it.

[5] MakeUseOf.com: How Do Celebrities Manage Their Social Media Accounts And What Can We Learn From Them.

[6] Tribune.com.pk: Social media 'more addictive than cigarettes and alcohol'.

[7] Jad-journal.com: Social media use and anxiety in emerging adults.

[8] MDPI.com: Online Social Networking and Addiction—A Review of the Psychological Literature.

[9] Adaa.org: Social Media Obsession and Anxiety.

[10] Crunch.WinfiY.com: Meet the Most Famous Dog in the World of Social Media!

[11] Mediakix.com: How Much Time Do People Spend On Social Media?

[12] MediaKix.com: Mediakix | Influencer Marketing Agency.

[13] WinfiY crunch: Make your day of 26 Hours. Here is How.

[14] KPCB.com: 2018 Internet Trends Report by Kleiner Perkins Caufield Byers.

[15] TechCrunch.com: U.S. Consumers Now Spend More Time In Apps Than Watching TV.

[16] VICE.com: Your Addiction to Social Media Is No Accident.

[17] Independent.co.uk: Man Who Invented 'Like' Button Deletes Facebook App Over Addiction Fears.

[18] Inc.com: The Surprising Reason Millennials Check Their Phones 150 Times a Day.

[19] Crunch.WinfiY.com: This is Why You can't ignore Social Media & Your Smartphone's Bloody Push Notifications!

[20] Crunch.WinfiY.com: Why You Find It So Hard To Delete Fucking Facebook!

[21] Wikipedia.org: Children's Online Privacy Protection Act.

[22] TheGuardian.com: Are smartphones really making our children sad?

[23] Crunch.WinfiY.com: 25% of Children Under Six Have Their Own Smartphone & Here Is More Shocking Fact!

[24] AAP.org: American Academy of Pediatrics Announces New Recommendations for Children's Media Use.

[25] FTC.gov: Children's Online Privacy Protection Rule ("COPPA").

[26] Mottnpch.org: Parents on social media: Likes and dislikes of sharenting.

[27] BBC.co.uk: 'Sharenting': Are you OK with what your parents post?

[28] NYtimes.com: New Facebook App for Children Ignites Debate Among Families.

[29] NYtimes.com: Turn Off Messenger Kids, Health Experts Plead to Facebook.

[30] ScienceDaily.com: Screen-addicted teens are unhappy.

[31] Wikipedia.org: Fear of Missing Out.

[32] Time.com: This Is The Best Way to Overcome Fear of Missing Out.

[33] ROLLZIGN.com: Best News Apps & Websites to keep You Always Updated.

[34] Mashable.com: Chinese woman goes blind after playing China's most addictive mobile game for an entire day.

[35] WebMD.com: Prevent Eyestrain From Digital Devices.

[36] BestHealthMag.ca: How Social Media Is Ruining Your Sleep.

[37] FastCompany.com: Why Your Free Time Probably Shouldn't Be Screen Time.

[38] FastCompany.com: Maybe It's Time To Regulate Gadgets And Apps Like Cigarettes.

[39] Independent.co.uk: Heavy Social Media Users 'Trapped In Endless Cycle Of Depression'.

[40] Google.com: Narcissism.

[41] TheAtlantic.com: Have Smartphones Destroyed a Generation?

[42] Crunch.WinfiY.com: Is Social Media making you Unhappy?

[43] Tonic.vice.com: Is Social Media Making Us Unhappy?

[44] Crunch.WinfiY.com: Attention students! You focus standby time is 3 minutes only!

[45] Crunch.WinfiY.com: Just don't look at Your Smartphone and this App will Pay You!

[46] Wikipedia: Cyberbullying.

[47] Stopbullying.gov: What Is Cyberbullying.

[48] Kidshealth.org: Cyberbullying.

[49] KidsLiveSafe.com: The Real Numbers and Increasing Online Dangers.

[50] KidsLiveSafe.com: The Real Numbers and Increasing Online Dangers.

[51] TheGuardian.com: Online harassment of women at risk of becoming 'established norm', study finds.

[52] Time.com: You Asked: Is Social Media Making Me Miserable?

[53] IndiaToday.in: Indian-origin boy in UK committed suicide after cyber bullying by classmates.

[54] MeganMeierFoundation.org: Bullying, Cyberbullying & Suicide Statistics.

[55] Prevnet.ca: Legal Consequences of Cyberbullying.

[56] Blogs.PsychCentral.com: 6 Steps for Dealing with Adult Bullies.

[57] WinfiY crunch: How Your Smartphone Affect Your Intelligence?

[58] MedicalDaily.com: Smart Phone, Dumb Human: 5 Ways Technology Is Reducing Your Overall Intelligence.

[59] PsychologyToday.com: 6 Reasons Why Selfie-Taking Can Be Hazardous to Your Health.

[60] WashingtonPost.com: More people died taking selfies in India last year than anywhere else in the world.

[61] Mirror.co.uk: Teenager leapt in front of Tube train after taking selfie called 'last pic before I die' inquest hears.

[62] TheAtlantic.com: Have Smartphones Destroyed a Generation?

[63] BusinessInsider.in: A 26-year-old woman racked up $10,000 of debt after trying to become an 'Instagram star' - and it reveals a huge issue with the platform.

[64] CIO.com: Social Media Costs -- and Some Workers Are Paying With Their Jobs.

[65] WinfiY crunch: This Country Is Planning To Tax Its Social Media Users!

[66] TheConversation.com: What happens when people lose trust in the Internet?

[67] JeffBullas.com: How to Beat Distractions and Skyrocket Your Productivity.

[68] CareerBuilder.com: CareerBuilder Study Reveals Top Ten Productivity Killers at Work.

[69] WinfiY crunch: Cost of distractions: 25 minutes each!

[70] Zapier.com: 14 Tools to Help You Avoid Distractions and Stay Focused at Work.

[71] www.news.com.au: Man kills victim live on Facebook and goes on the run after posting 'Easter day slaughter' video.

[72] abc7chicago.com: Hate crime, kidnapping charges filed against 4 in Facebook Live torture case.

[73] Crunch.WinfiY.com: Is Internet Addictive?

[74] Crunch.WinfiY.com: How Many Pages Are There On The Internet ('or Google')?

[75] BoredPanda.com: Somebody Noticed Donald Trump's Chin Looks Like A Frog, And Now People Can't Stop Trolling Him.

[76] BBC.com: Internet trolls face up to two years in jail under new laws.

[77] WinfiY crunch: Why Boredom Is Necessary (Especially For Youngsters)?

[78] WinfiY crunch: Want to maximize Your creativity? Just Relax; Sit Idle & Do Nothing! Here is Why.

[79] Blog.dscout.com: Putting a Finger on Our Phone Obsession.

[80] CNN.com: Smartphone addiction could be changing your brain.

[81] Crunch.WinfiY.com: Do You own Your Phone or Does Your Phone Own You?

[82] Play.Google.com: SPACE - Break phone addiction - Apps on Google Play.

[83] Economictimes.indiatimes.com: Mobile has become the new babysitter! Smartphone addiction cases up by 75% in one year.

[84] Helpguide.org: Smartphone Addiction.

[85] Journals.uchicago.edu: Brain Drain: The Mere Presence of One's Own Smartphone Reduces Available Cognitive Capacity.

[86] CNN.com: Smartphone addiction could be changing your brain.

[87] BusinessInsider.in: Bill Gates and Steve Jobs shared a surprising philosophy about tech - and it should have been a big red flag.

[88] TheSun.co.uk: Why your smartphone may be making you sad.

[89] WinfiY crunch: Cost of distractions: 25 minutes each!

[90] APA.org: What You Need to Know about Willpower: The Psychological Science of Self-Control.

[91] LifeHacker.com: Change Your Screen to Grayscale to Combat Phone Addiction.

[92] Business2Community.com : 10 Colors That Increase Sales, and Why Read more.

[93] WinfiY crunch: Want to maximize Your creativity? Just Relax; Sit Idle & Do Nothing! Here is Why.

[94] WinfiY crunch: Want To Achieve Your Goals? Write Them! Here Is Why.

[95] Pixabay.com: Man Office Businessman.

[96] Crunch.WinfiY.com: Why Multi-tasking feels so good & why you should avoid it?

[97] WinfiY crunch: Stick to Single-Tasking & Get More Done!

[98] Crunch.WinfiY.com: This little (absolutely free!) thing can add 3 years to Your Life!

[99] WinfiY crunch: When You Should NOT Post Your Vacation Pics On Social Media?

[100] Crunch.WinfiY.com: How much (or how little!) do you read online?

[101] WinfiY crunch: How Much Do You Read Before Sharing? Let's Check Your Smartness!

[102] Forbes.com: 59 Percent Of You Will Share This Article Without Even Reading It.

[103] WinfiY crunch: Why You Need To Take Care of Your Children's Gaming Habits?

[104] TheSun.co.uk: GAME OVER Girl, 9, in 'rehab after getting hooked playing Fortnite for 10 hours a day and wets herself to avoid switching off'.

[105] Dailymail.co.uk: Social media and cell phones are so stressful that we now need MORE than 8 hours sleep, expert says.

[106] WinfiY crunch: If Sleep Were A Credit Card Company, Many Of Us Would Be Indebted!

[107] WinfiY crunch: Make your day of 26 Hours. Here is How.

[108] Crunch.WinfiY.com: Don't Read E-Books at Sleep Time. Here is why!

[109] Crunch.WinfiY.com: Stop Using Smartphone Near Sleep Time! Here is Why...

[110] Crunch.WinfiY.com: You Need A Bedtime Alarm For A Good Sleep!

[111] Crunch.WinfiY.com: Say No to Music! But Why?

[112] www.Recode.net: People spend almost as much time on Instagram as they do on Facebook.

[113] Siva Vaidhyanathan's Antisocial Media: How Facebook Disconnects Us and Undermines Democracy.

[114] Wired.com: Facebook Exposed 87 Million Users to Cambridge Analytica.

[115] Crunch.WinfiY.com: How many Facebook Users Are Going To Delete Facebook?

[116] Crunch.WinfiY.com: What happens on Facebook in one Minute? (It's Alarming!).

[117] Liebertpub.com: The Facebook Experiment: Quitting Facebook Leads to Higher Levels of Well-Being.

[118] Pixabay.com: Facebook Social Media Addiction.

[119] Independent.co.uk: Man Who Invented 'Like' Button Deletes Facebook App Over Addiction Fears.

[120] TinyAmbitions.com: The Best I've done to Simplify My 'Social' Life.

[121] WinfiY crunch: Is Facebook Popularity Going Down & Should You Join The Trend?

[122] Siva Vaidhyanathan's Antisocial Media: How Facebook Disconnects Us and Undermines Democracy.

[123] Independent.co.uk: Instagram ranked as having the worst effect on young people's mental health, report finds.

[124] WashingtonPost.com: More people died taking selfies in India last year than anywhere else in the world.

[125] The Conversation: How parents and teens can reduce the impact of social media on youth well-being.

[126] Wellbeing.Google: Our commitment to Digital Wellbeing | Google.

[127] TheVerge.com: In a leaked memo, Facebook executive describes the consequences of its growth-at-all-costs mentality.

[128] TechCrunch.com: Facebook knows literally everything about you.
[129] TechCrunch.com: Terms And Conditions Are The Biggest Lie Of Our Industry.
[130] Fortune.com: This Is the Personal Data that Facebook Collects—And Sometimes Sells.
[131] Wired.com: Why Zuckerberg's 14-Year Apology Tour Hasn't Fixed Facebook.
[132] BeInternetAwesome.withgoogle.com: Be Internet Awesome.
[133] Kids.YouTube.com: YouTube Kids.
[134] AndroidAuthority.com: Android Dashboard, Shush mode, and App Timers will help you take charge of your 'digital wellbeing'.
[135] Time.com: Apple's New Software Will Help You Use Your Phone Less Often.
[136] TheGuardian.com: Apple's new 'digital wellbeing' tools aim to help reduce screen time.
[137] Cnet.com: Google, Android P take on phone addiction with Android Dashboard.
[138] BBC.com: Wetherspoon pub chain shuts its social media accounts.
[139] Wired.com: Facebook Exposed 87 Million Users to Cambridge Analytica.
[140] NYTimes.com: How Trump Consultants Exploited the Facebook Data of Millions.
[141] Blog.Mozilla.org: Mozilla Presses Pause on Facebook Advertising.
[142] Blog.Mozilla.org: Mozilla Statement, Petition: Facebook and Cambridge Analytica.
[143] FastCompany.com: A Brief History Of Mark Zuckerberg Apologizing (Or Not Apologizing) For Stuff.
[144] Twitter.com: Brian Acton Status ID: 976231995846963201.
[145] Independent.co.uk: Man Who Invented 'Like' Button Deletes Facebook App Over Addiction Fears.
[146] Independent.co.uk: Instagram ranked as having the worst effect on young people's mental health, report finds.
[147] TheGuardian.com: 'Our minds can be hijacked': the tech insiders who fear a smartphone dystopia.
[148] TheGuardian.com: Ex-Facebook president Sean Parker: site made to exploit human 'vulnerability'.
[149] TheVerge.com: In 2017, Key Facebook Builders Disowned Their Creation.
[150] Wired.com: Tech Bigwigs Know How Addictive Their Products Are. Why Don't the Rest of Us?
[151] CNBC.com: Facebook should be regulated like a cigarette company, says Salesforce CEO.

[152] BuzzFeed.com: George Soros Just Launched A Scathing Attack On Google And Facebook.

[153] FastCompany.com: Maybe It's Time To Regulate Gadgets And Apps Like Cigarettes.

[154] Time.com: You Asked: Is Social Media Making Me Miserable?

[155] BuzzFeed.com: Growth At Any Cost: Top Facebook Executive Defended Data Collection In 2016 Memo — And Warned That Facebook Could Get People Killed.

[156] BestHealthMag.ca: How Social Media Is Ruining Your Sleep.

[157] TheGuardian.com: I was one of Facebook's first users. I shouldn't have trusted Mark Zuckerberg.

[158] Wired.com: Turn Off Your Push Notifications. All of Them.

[159] TheVerge.com: Former Facebook exec says social media is ripping apart society.

[160] AAP.org: American Academy of Pediatrics Announces New Recommendations for Children's Media Use.

[161] Crunch.WinfiY.com: Right to Disconnect! Freedom For Not Replying to Emails, Calls & Messages!

[162] FastCompany.com: Should It Be Illegal For Your Boss To Make You Email After Work?

[163] QZ.com: Uganda plans to tax social media to stop gossip on Facebook, WhatsApp, Twitter.

[164] WinfiY crunch: This Country Is Planning To Tax Its Social Media Users!

[165] MTN.co.ug: Internet OTT Services.

[166] QZ.com: Zambia is the latest African state trying to muzzle social media with arbitrary laws.